OTEE STUDY GUIDE AND PRACTICE TEST FOR CBSA (2024-25)

MASTER THE CANADIAN BORDER SERVICES OTEE CBSA EXAMS WITH COMPREHENSIVE PRACTICE TESTS AND STUDY STRATEGIES

DR. FANATOMY
★★★★★

copyright@ dr. fanatomy 2024

All rights reserved. No part of this publication may be reproduced, distributed, or transmitted in any form or by any means, including photocopying, recording, or other electronic or mechanical methods, without the prior written permission of the publisher, except in the case of brief quotations embodied in critical reviews and certain other noncommercial uses permitted by copyright law.

This book is a work of non-fiction, and any resemblance to actual persons, living or dead, or actual events is purely coincidental.

The information and techniques described in this book are intended for educational and informational purposes only. The author and publisher shall not be held liable for any injury, damage, or loss arising from using or misusing the information presented in this book.

While every effort has been made to ensure the accuracy of the information contained within this book, the author and publisher make no warranties or representations express or implied, about the completeness, accuracy, reliability, suitability, or availability with respect to the contents of this book for any purpose. The use of any information provided in this book is at the reader's own risk.

DECLARATION

The author of this book, OTEE Practice Test and Study Guide for CBSA: Master the Canadian Border Services OTEE CBSA Exams with Comprehensive Practice Tests and Study Strategies, has no affiliation with or endorsement from the Canadian Border Services Agency (CBSA) or any other official authority.

This book is an independent exam preparation guide designed to assist candidates in studying and preparing for the CBSA OTEE exams. It is intended solely as an educational resource and should not be considered an official source of information or certification for the exam.

TABLE OF CONTENTS

1. ABOUT THE EXAM - AN INTRODUCTION (Pg:4-11)

- Introduction
- Exam Overview
- Competencies Assessed
- Alternate Test Dates
- Accommodations
- Exam Results
- Exam Structure and Format
- Competencies Assessed by the OTEE

2. PREPARATION STRATEGIES (Pg: 12-18)

- Preparation Strategies
- Creating a Study Plan
- Effective Study Techniques
- Utilizing Practice Tests
- Analyzing Practice Test Results for Improvement
- Practice Test Analysis and Time Management
- Preparing for the Canadian Border Services Entrance Test (OTEE)
- Additional Requirements for CBSA Officers

3. REASONING SKILLS (Pg: 19-38)

- Introduction to Reasoning Skills
- Importance:
- Logical Deduction:
- Critical Thinking:
- Problem-Solving:
- Relevance
- Types of Reasoning Questions in the OTEE
- Sample Questions and Explanations
- (A) Logical Deduction Questions
- (B) Critical Thinking Questions
- (C) Problem-Solving Questions
- (D) Inference Questions

4. ANALYTICAL THINKING (Pg: 39-57)

- Introduction to Analytical Thinking
- Understanding the Types of Analytical Thinking Questions
- Strategies to Approach Analytical Problems
- Practice with Examples and Sample Questions
- (A) Logical Reasoning Questions
- (B) Pattern Recognition
- (C) Problem-Solving
- (D) Data Interpretation

TABLE OF CONTENTS

5. CLIENT SERVICE ORIENTATION (Pg:58 - 72)

- Importance of Client Service Orientation for CBSA Officers
- Understanding the Types of Client Service Orientation Questions
- Strategies to Approach Client Service Orientation Problems
- Practice with Examples and Sample Questions
- (A) Scenario-Based Question
- (B) Prioritization and Decision Making
- (C) Communication Skills

6. WRITING SKILLS (Pg: 73 - 90)

- Introduction to Writing Skills
- Why Writing Skills Are Important for CBSA Officers:
- Types of Writing Skills Questions
- Approach to Solving Writing Skills Questions
- Practice with Examples and Sample Questions
- (A) Sentence Structure and Word Arrangement
- (B) Grammar and Syntax
- (C) Clarity and Precision
- (D) Report Writing
- (E) Tone and Audience
- (F) Proofreading and Editing
- (G) Document Completion

7. PRACTICE TEST (Pg: 91-109)

- (A) Reasoning Skills Practice Questions
- (B) Analytical Thinking Practice Questions
- (C) Client Service Orientation Practice Questions
- (D) Writing skills Practice Questions

PRACTICE TEST ANSWERS (Pg: 110-116)

CONCLUSION (Pg: 117)

1. About the Exam - An Introduction

Introduction

The Officer Trainee Entrance Exam (OTEE) is a crucial initial step in becoming an officer trainee at the Canada Border Services Agency (CBSA). The Officer Trainee Entrance Exam (OTEE) is crucial in the selection process for becoming a Canada Border Services Agency (CBSA) officer trainee. It is designed to assess competencies essential to effectively perform CBSA duties.

The OTEE consists of 117 multiple-choice questions, which candidates must complete within 135 minutes. This chapter will provide a detailed overview of the exam structure, the competencies assessed, and effective preparation strategies.

Exam Overview

- **Format**: The OTEE is an online exam consisting of 117 multiple-choice questions.

- **Content:** The questions are hypothetical and do not require prior knowledge of the CBSA.

- **Duration**: Once started, the exam must be completed within 135 minutes. Candidates have one week to complete it.

Competencies Assessed

- **Reasoning Skills**: Drawing conclusions or inferences from information to solve problems.

- **Analytical Thinking**: The ability to logically break down and work through situations or problems to arrive at outcomes.

- **Client Service Orientation**: The ability to provide high-quality service to internal and external clients, focusing on quality, timeliness, knowledge, courtesy, and fairness.

- **Writing Skills**: The ability to produce clear, correct written documents using plain language in a style appropriate to the intended audience.

Alternate Test Dates

- Requests for an alternate test date will be considered for the following reasons:

    - Religious Obligations
    - Death in the Immediate Family
    - Medical Reasons: Must be supported by a doctor's certificate proving illness for the entire week.
    - Planned Vacation: Costs must have already been incurred.
    - Paid Military Leave or Training

- Proof is required for these circumstances, and candidates must notify the CBSA via the web form provided in the test invitation.

Accommodations

- Candidates with functional limitations, disabilities, or conditions that may impede test performance should notify the CBSA's National Recruitment Team before beginning the exam.

- If a physical or psychological problem arises before the exam, candidates must notify the CBSA immediately via the link in their invitation.

- Proceeding with the exam without prior accommodation requests means accepting the exam results as final.

Exam Results

- **Successful Results**: Valid indefinitely.

- **Unsuccessful Results**: Termination of candidacy. Reapplication is allowed one year after the initial attempt.

- If the test is retaken before the one-year waiting period, the new results will be invalid, and a new waiting period will commence from the retake date.

Misconduct

- Cheating and plagiarism are strictly prohibited.

- Violations, including assisting others in cheating, may result in removal from the selection process and other sanctions.

This guide provides a thorough overview of the OTEE, helping candidates prepare for the exam by understanding the format, assessed competencies, and procedures for alternate dates, accommodations, and handling results.

Exam Structure and Format

Online Exam Overview

- Number of Questions: 117 multiple-choice questions.
- Duration: 135 minutes.
- Completion Requirement: The exam must be completed in one sitting; candidates have one week to complete it once it is started.

Hypothetical Questions

- The questions are designed to assess competencies without requiring specific prior knowledge of the CBSA. They are hypothetical in nature, focusing on general skills and abilities.

Example Question Structure

- **Question Type: Multiple-choice**

Example:

"A passenger at the airport expresses dissatisfaction with the customs process. How should you respond to ensure a positive client service experience?"

- *A) Explain the process in detail, including all legal requirements.*
- *B) Listen to the passenger's concerns and provide a polite and informed response.*
- *C) Refer the passenger to a supervisor without attempting to address the issue.*
- *D) Ignore the passenger's complaint, as it is not within your jurisdiction.*

Correct Answer: *B) Listen to the passenger's concerns and provide a polite and informed response.*

Competencies Assessed by the OTEE

Reasoning Skills

- **Definition:** The ability to draw conclusions or inferences from information to solve problems.
- **Importance:** Critical for decision-making and problem-solving in dynamic situations.

Example:

A cargo shipment's documents are incomplete. As a CBSA officer, how would you proceed?

- *A) Allow the shipment to pass and request the missing documents later.*
- *B) Detain the shipment and contact the sender for further information.*
- *C) Refuse the shipment entry and notify the authorities.*
- *D) Ignore the missing documents, as they are not crucial.*

- *Correct Answer: B) Detain the shipment and contact the sender for further information.*

Tips for Improvement:

- Practice logic puzzles and critical thinking exercises.
- Engage in activities that require problem-solving under time constraints.

Analytical Thinking

- **Definition**: The ability to use a logical thought process to analyze a situation or problem and arrive at an outcome.
- **Importance**: Necessary for understanding complex information and making informed decisions.

Example:

A passenger presents a passport that appears slightly altered. What steps should you take?

- *A) Assume the alteration is minor and allow entry.*
- *B) Detain the passenger and confiscate the passport without explanation.*
- *C) Question the passenger about the passport's origin and cross-check with records.*
- *D) Ignore the issue and proceed with standard processing.*

Correct Answer: C) Question the passenger about the passport's origin and cross-check with records.

Tips for Improvement:

- Engage in case studies and scenario analyses.
- Break down complex information into smaller, manageable parts.

Client Service Orientation

Definition: The ability to provide high-quality service to internal and external clients, focusing on quality, timeliness, knowledge, courtesy, and fairness.

Importance: Ensures positive interactions with the public and maintains the CBSA's reputation.

Example:

An elderly traveler is confused about customs procedures. How should you assist them?

- A) Direct them to a general information board.
- B) Provide a quick explanation and move on to the next traveler.
- C) Explain, assist with forms, and ensure they understand the process.
- D) Ignore the situation as it's not within your duties.

Correct Answer: C) Offer a detailed explanation, assist with forms, and ensure they understand the process.

Tips for Improvement:

- Develop active listening skills.
- Practice empathy and patience in customer service scenarios.

Writing Skills

- **Definition**: The ability to produce clear, correct written documents, including correspondence, reports, and other documentation, using plain language.

- **Importance**: Essential for accurate record-keeping, communication, and reporting.

Example:

- Write a brief incident report detailing a passenger's failure to declare goods.

Sample Response:

"On 17th January 2024, at 7.15 p.m., a passenger identified as Mark James was found with undeclared goods in their possession. The items included a small knife. The passenger was informed of their obligation to declare all items and the potential penalties for failure. A formal report was filed, and the items were confiscated."

Tips for Improvement:

- Practice writing concise, clear, and grammatically correct documents.
- Focus on structuring information logically and effectively.

Conclusion

This chapter provides an overview of the OTEE, including its structure, format, and the competencies it assesses. Understanding these elements is crucial for effective preparation. The following chapters will delve into specific study strategies, practice tests, and exam-day tips to ensure you are well-prepared for success.

Competency	Description	Importance	Example Question
Reasoning Skills	Drawing conclusions or inferences from information to solve problems.	Crucial for decision-making and problem-solving.	Handling incomplete cargo shipment documents.
Analytical Thinking	Using a logical thought process to break down and work through a situation or problem to arrive at an outcome.	Important for understanding complex information.	Responding to a suspiciously altered passport.
Client Service Orientation	Providing high-quality service to clients, focusing on quality, timeliness, knowledge, courtesy, and fairness.	Ensures positive public interactions.	Assisting a confused elderly traveler with customs procedures.
Writing Skills	Producing clear, correct written documents using plain language.	Essential for accurate communication and records.	Writing an incident report for undeclared goods.

2. Preparation Strategies

Preparation Strategies

To effectively prepare for the Officer Trainee Entrance Exam (OTEE), a structured approach, a study plan, various study techniques, and practice tests are required. This chapter provides detailed strategies to assist candidates in excelling in the exam, offering practical examples at each step.

Creating a Study Plan

Setting Study Goals and Timelines

- **Defining Clear Objectives**: Start by identifying specific goals for each competency. For instance, I aim to improve my reasoning skills by focusing on logical puzzles and pattern recognition.

- **Resources for Studying**: Gather materials such as textbooks, online courses, and official study guides from CBSA. For example, use "Mastering Analytical Thinking" as a textbook for developing analytical thinking skills.

- **Extended Study Timeline**: A three-month recommended study timeline allows for in-depth coverage of all competencies.

Sample Three-Month Study Schedule

Month	Competency Focus	Activities	Milestones
1	Reasoning Skills	Study logic puzzles, practice pattern recognition questions	Complete 200 logic puzzles
2	Analytical Thinking	Analyze case studies, practice data interpretation	Analyze 10 case studies
3	Client Service Orientation	Role-playing scenarios, studying CBSA customer service policies	Respond to 15 service scenarios
4	Writing Skills	Practice essay writing, review grammar rules	Write 5 sample essays
5	Review & Practice Tests	Full-length practice exams	Complete 3 timed practice tests

Balancing Study Time Across Competencies

- **Assessing Proficiency:** Evaluate your skills using self-assessment quizzes or practice tests. For instance, take a practice test initially and review your score to identify areas for improvement.

- **Adjusting Focus:** Dedicate more time to the skills in which you are less proficient. For example, if a practice test shows that you need improvement in analytical thinking, schedule additional study sessions for that area.

Incorporating Practice Tests into Your Schedule

- **Variety in Practice Tests:** Use both topic-specific and full-length practice tests. For instance, after studying client service orientation, take a practice test focusing only on customer service scenarios, followed by a comprehensive test that includes all competencies.

Effective Study Techniques

Active Reading and Note-Taking

- **Active Reading:** Engage with the material by asking questions, summarizing sections, and highlighting key points.

- **Note-Taking Methods:**

- **Outlining**: Structure notes in a hierarchical format with headings and subheadings.
- **Mind Mapping**: Visualize connections between concepts using diagrams.
- **Example**: For client service orientation, create a mind map with "Empathy," "Communication," and "Problem-Solving" as the main branches.

Memorization Techniques

- **Mnemonics:** Create memory aids, such as "RACE" (Reasoning, Analytical thinking, Client service, and Effective writing), to remember key competencies.

- **Spaced Repetition:** Regularly review information at increasing intervals to reinforce memory.

Critical Thinking and Problem-Solving Exercises

- **Real-World Scenarios**: Practice analyzing real-life situations relevant to CBSA duties.
    - **Example**: Scenario: A traveler becomes irate at customs. Analyze the best way to defuse the situation while maintaining security protocols.
- **Group Discussions:** Join study groups to discuss and debate different perspectives on ethical dilemmas or complex cases.

Study Techniques and Examples

Technique	Description	Example
Active Reading	Engaging with text through questioning and summarizing	Highlight key client service principles
Note-Taking Methods	Outlining, mind mapping	Mind map for client service concepts
Mnemonics	Memory aids for lists or concepts	"RACE" for competencies
Spaced Repetition	Reviewing information at increasing intervals	Flashcards for key terms
Real-World Scenarios	Analyzing and discussing real-life situations	Handling an irate traveler
Group Discussions	Exploring complex topics through study group debates	Ethical dilemma discussions

Utilizing Practice Tests

Importance of Practice Tests

- **Familiarization with Exam Format**: Regular practice tests help candidates understand the structure and time constraints of the OTEE.

- **Assessment and Adjustment:** Use practice test results to identify knowledge gaps and adjust study plans accordingly.

How to Simulate Exam Conditions

- **Creating a Realistic Environment:** Find a quiet space, use a timer, and minimize interruptions. Practice under timed conditions to build exam stamina and time management skills.

    - **Example**: Allocate 135 minutes for a full-length practice test, mirroring the actual exam duration.

Analyzing Practice Test Results for Improvement

- **Reviewing Answers**: Thoroughly analyze correct and incorrect responses to understand the rationale behind each answer.
    - **Example**: If a candidate frequently misses questions on analytical thinking, they should focus on dissecting complex scenarios and understanding underlying principles.

- **Time Management Strategies**: Practice allocating specific time blocks for different test sections. For instance, aim to complete reasoning skills questions within 30 minutes to allow more time for analytical thinking and writing tasks.

Practice Test Analysis and Time Management

Aspect	Action	Purpose
Reviewing Answers	Analyze correct and incorrect responses	Understand reasoning and correct misunderstandings
Identifying Patterns	Note recurring errors	Target specific weaknesses
Time Management	Allocate specific times for each section	Improve pacing and time allocation

Developing a solid preparation strategy for the OTEE is essential. Setting study goals, using various techniques, and taking practice tests helps build a strong understanding of the exam content. Real-world scenarios and diverse practice formats enhance critical thinking, while analyzing test results helps refine study efforts. With careful planning and preparation, candidates can confidently approach the OTEE and achieve their desired outcomes.

Preparing for the Canadian Border Services Entrance Test (OTEE)

Considering a Career with the Canadian Border Services?

Ask yourself the following questions:

- Relocation: Are you willing to relocate?
- Work Hours: Can you work shifts, including weekends and statutory holidays?
- Handling Firearms: Are you comfortable with firearms and other defensive equipment?
- Diverse Interactions: Are you comfortable working with people from different cultures, backgrounds, and lifestyles?

Work Environment

- CBSA agents work at airports, land, and marine borders. The work can be busy, sometimes in bad weather and confined spaces.

CBSA Practice Questions

- Online Practice Tests: Practice questions for the OTEE are available online.
- Free Quiz: Try a free quiz to test your knowledge.

Border Services Test – Officer Trainee Entrance Exam (OTEE)

Exam Sections

- Reasoning and Analytical Thinking
- Prioritizing Tasks
- Client Service
- Writing

Interview Assessment

The interview will evaluate:
- Handling of difficult situations

- Communication skills
- Decisiveness
- Professional judgment
- Values, integrity, and ethics

Additional Requirements for CBSA Officers

Firearms Training
- Completing the Canadian Firearms Safety Course (CFSC) and the Canadian Restricted Firearms Safety Course (CRFSC) is required.

Physical Fitness Evaluation
- Must complete the Physical Ability Requirement Evaluation (PARE), which includes:
    - Push-pull and weight-carry
    - Obstacle course

- **Test results are provided immediately and are valid for 18 months.**

Psychological Assessment
- Conducted by a psychologist, involving a written test and an interview.

Medical Assessment
- Conducted by a physician to ensure adequate vision and hearing. Includes a 'use of force' test.

Security Clearance
- A complete security check is mandatory.

3. Reasoning Skills

Introduction to Reasoning Skills

Overview

Importance:

- **Decision-Making**: Crucial for making sound decisions in real-time situations.
- **Problem-Solving**: Enables effective resolution of complex issues in border security.

Application:

- Judgment: Used to assess the legitimacy of travel documents and travelers' intentions.

Examples:

- **Example 1**: A CBSA officer detects discrepancies in a traveler's visa and cross-checks with a database to verify authenticity.
- **Example 2**: During an inspection, an officer notices unusual cargo manifest details and uses reasoning skills to determine the necessity of a deeper investigation.

Definition

- **Concept**: The cognitive ability to analyze, infer, and conclude from information.

Components:

(1) Logical Deduction:

- Definition: Identifying patterns and relationships.
- Example: Inferring a potential connection between an expired visa and suspicious behavior.

(2) Critical Thinking:

- Definition: Evaluating arguments and discerning the relevance of information.
- Example: Assessing the validity of an explanation given by a traveler under interrogation.

(3) Problem-Solving:

- Definition: Using structured thinking to resolve issues.
- Example: Determining the best course of action when handling a group of asylum seekers.

Component	Definition	Example
Logical Deduction	Identifying patterns and relationships	Inferring connections in data inconsistencies
Critical Thinking	Evaluating arguments and discerning relevance	Assessing explanations provided by travelers
Problem-Solving	Using structured thinking to resolve issues	Deciding on procedures for handling complex cases

Relevance

(1) Day-to-Day Application:

- **Truthfulness:** Determining the accuracy of information provided by travelers.

- **Risk Assessment**: Identifying potential threats or illegal activities.

- **Example**: An officer uses reasoning to decide whether a traveler's nervous behavior indicates a potential security risk or is merely a result of anxiety.

(2) High-Pressure Situations:

- **Quick Decisions:** Making prompt and accurate decisions in busy environments.
- **Clarity and Composure**: Maintaining a calm and professional demeanor under stress.
- **Example**: During a security alert, officers use reasoning skills to efficiently evacuate a checkpoint while ensuring the safety of all involved.

Situation	Skill Applied	Example
Assessing travel documents	Critical Thinking	Verifying discrepancies in visas
Identifying suspicious cargo	Logical Deduction	Noticing unusual patterns in cargo manifests
Handling security alerts	Problem-Solving	Coordinating an efficient checkpoint evacuation

Summary

- **Purpose:** Enhancing the ability to serve the public, maintain order, and protect borders.
- **Outcome**: Improved decision-making and operational effectiveness, ensuring a secure and orderly border environment.

Types of Reasoning Questions in the OTEE

(A) Logical Deduction Questions

Description

Logical deduction questions evaluate the ability to recognize patterns, relationships, or sequences to make logical conclusions. This skill is essential for CBSA officers to understand complex scenarios and make well-informed decisions.

Examples

- Example 1: Identify the next item in a sequence based on a given pattern.

- Example 2: Determine the relationship between different entities (e.g., if all A are B, and all B are C, what can we infer about A and C?).

Sample Questions and Explanations

1) Question: Consider the sequence: 2, 4, 8, 16, __. What is the next number?

- Options: A) 20, B) 24, C) 32, D) 64
- Explanation: The sequence doubles each time. The next number is 16×2=32
- Correct Answer: C) 32

2) Question: If all cats are animals, and all animals have four legs, what can we infer about cats?

- Options: A) Cats are mammals, B) Cats are reptiles, C) Cats have four legs, D) Cats can fly
- Explanation: Since all cats are animals and all animals have four legs, it follows that all cats have four legs.
- Correct Answer: C) Cats have four legs

3) Question: Given the pattern: 5, 10, 20, 40, __, what is the next number?

- Options: A) 50, B) 60, C) 70, D) 80
- Explanation: The sequence multiplies by 2. Thus, 40×2=80
- Correct Answer: D) 80

4) Question: If all squares are rectangles, and some rectangles are blue, can we conclude that all squares are blue?

- Options: A) Yes, B) No, C) Cannot be determined
- Explanation: The statement "some rectangles are blue" does not imply that all rectangles or all squares are blue. Thus, we cannot conclude that all squares are blue.
- Correct Answer: B) No

Sample Questions and Explanations

5) Question: In a code, the word "HOUSE" is written as "IPVTF." How will the word "LIGHT" be written in that code?

- *Options: A) MJHIU, B) MJHGU, C) MJHJW, D) MJIHV*
- *Explanation: The pattern adds 1 to each letter's position in the alphabet. L + 1 = M, I + 1 = J, G + 1 = H, H + 1 = I, T + 1 = U. Thus, "LIGHT" becomes "MJHIU."*
- *Correct Answer: A) MJHIU*

6) Question: If "Many birds can fly" and "Penguins are birds," can we conclude that penguins can fly?

- *Options: A) Yes, B) No, C) Maybe, D) None of the above*
- *Explanation: The statement "Many birds can fly" doesn't say all of them can fly. Thus, we cannot conclude that penguins can fly.*
- *Correct Answer: B) No*

7) Question: Find the missing term in the series: 3, 6, 11, 18, __, 38.

- *Options: A) 25, B) 27, C) 29, D) 31*
- *Explanation: The pattern increases by consecutive odd numbers: +3, +5, +7, +9, +11. So, the next number after 18 is 18+09 =27.*
- *Correct Answer: B) 27*

8) Question: If some A are B, and all B are C, which of the following is true?

- *Options: A) Some A are C, B) No A are C, C) All A are C, D) None of the above*
- *Explanation: If some A are B, and all B are C, then some A are necessarily C.*
- *Correct Answer: A) Some A are C*

Sample Questions and Explanations

9) **Question: The sequence is: 21, 19, 17, 15, __. What comes next?**

- *Options: A) 13, B) 12, C) 11, D) 14*
- *Explanation: The sequence decreases by 2 each time. The next number is 15−2=1315 - 2 = 1315−2=13.*
- *Correct Answer: A) 13*

10) **Question: A code translates "APPLE" to "BQQMF." What is the translation for "BANANA"?**

- *Options: A) CBOBOB, B) CBPCNB, C) CBPDPB, D) CBPCPB*
- *Explanation: The code adds 1 to each letter's position in the alphabet. Thus, "BANANA" becomes "CBOBOB."*
- *Correct Answer: A) CBOBOB*

11) **Who is the tallest if A is taller than B and C is taller than A?**

- *Options: A) A, B) B, C) C, D) Cannot be determined*
- *Correct Answer: C) C*
- *Explanation: The given information states that C is taller than A, and A is taller than B, indicating that C is the tallest among them.*

12) **Question: If the statements "Some apples are red" and "All red fruits are sweet" are true, what can we conclude about some apples?**

- *Options: A) Some apples are not sweet, B) Some apples are sweet, C) All apples are red, D) Cannot be determined*
- *Correct Answer: B) Some apples are sweet*
- *Explanation: "Some apples are red" indicates at least some red apples. "All red fruits are sweet" implies that if a fruit is red, it must be sweet.*

All the answers and explanations provided are accurate. The reasoning skills involved in these questions include logical deduction and understanding hierarchical relationships, which are essential for the CBSA officer trainee role.

Types of Reasoning Questions in the OTEE

(B) Critical Thinking Questions

Description

Critical thinking questions assess a person's ability to evaluate arguments, identify assumptions, and discern the relevance of information. This skill is vital for CBSA officer trainees in making well-founded decisions based on credible information and reliable sources.

Examples

1. **Evaluating the Strength of an Argument**

   - **Description:** These questions ask you to analyze the logical coherence of an argument based on given premises. You may need to determine whether the conclusion logically follows from the premises or if the argument contains logical fallacies.

   - **Example:** If a person argues that "Since all border checks are time-consuming, increasing the number of officers will reduce wait times," you would evaluate whether the conclusion about reducing wait times logically follows the premise about border checks being time-consuming.

2. **Identifying Underlying Assumptions**

   - **Description:** This involves recognizing implicit assumptions that are not explicitly stated but are necessary for the argument to hold. Identifying these assumptions helps in evaluating the validity of the argument.

   - **Example:** In the statement "Enhanced surveillance cameras will reduce illegal activities at the border because people avoid places under surveillance," the underlying assumption is that individuals engaging in illegal activities are deterred by surveillance.

Practice Questions: Sample Questions Focusing on Critical Evaluation and Assumption Identification

1) The argument states, "If the economy improves, job opportunities will increase. The economy is improving, so job opportunities will increase."

- Options: A) The argument is strong, B) The argument is weak, C) The argument is irrelevant, D) Cannot determine
- Explanation: The argument is strong because the conclusion logically follows from the premise that an improving economy leads to more job opportunities.
- Correct Answer: A) The argument is strong

2) The statement, "If we install more lights in the parking lot, it will reduce crime because criminals prefer dark areas," is based on which assumption?

- Options: A) Criminals avoid areas with lights, B) Lights are expensive, C) The parking lot is currently dark, D) All crimes occur at night
- Explanation: The underlying assumption is that criminals are less likely to commit crimes in well-lit areas.
- Correct Answer: A) Criminals avoid areas with lights

3) "Implementing stricter immigration policies will reduce the number of illegal immigrants because fewer people will attempt to cross the border illegally." What is the assumption here?

- Options: A) Stricter policies are easy to implement, B) Stricter policies are effective at deterring illegal immigration, C) All immigrants are illegal, D) The current policies are not strict
- Explanation: The assumption is that stricter policies will effectively deter illegal immigration.
- Correct Answer: B) Stricter policies are effective at deterring illegal immigration

4) If an increase in the budget leads to better security measures and security measures have been improved, can we conclude that the budget has increased?

- Options: A) Yes, B) No, C) Maybe, D) Cannot determine
- Correct Answer: D) Cannot determine
- Explanation: Improved security measures could result from factors other than budget increases, like reallocating existing resources.

5) Question: "All reliable cars have good engines. This car has a good engine. Therefore, this car is reliable." Is this argument valid?

- Options: A) Yes, B) No, C) Cannot determine, D) Only if the car is new
- Correct Answer: B) No
- Explanation: The argument assumes that a good engine makes a car reliable, which may not be true as reliability also depends on other factors.

6) The premise is "All students who study hard pass their exams. John passed his exams." What assumption is made if we conclude that John studied hard?

- Options: A) John is intelligent, B) John studies hard, C) Passing exams require studying, D) All students pass exams
- Correct Answer: B) John studies hard
- Explanation: The conclusion assumes that because John passed, he must have studied hard, based on the given premise.

7) If "Increased border patrols reduce illegal crossings, and illegal crossings have decreased," what assumption supports the claim that the reduction is due to increased patrols?

- Options: A) Illegal crossings always decrease in winter, B) Increased patrols are the only factor, C) Economic conditions improved, D) No assumption
- Correct Answer: B) Increased patrols are the only factor
- Explanation: The argument assumes that other factors did not contribute to the decrease in illegal crossings.

8) **Question:** "Improving educational programs will lead to better job opportunities for graduates." What assumption does this statement rely on?

- Options: A) Educational programs are currently ineffective, B) Employers value educational qualifications, C) Job opportunities are scarce, D) Graduates are unemployed
- Correct Answer: B) Employers value educational qualifications
- Explanation: The statement assumes that employers consider educational improvements a hiring criterion.

9) **Question:** In the argument, "Reducing public transportation fares will increase ridership," what is the underlying assumption?

- Options: A) People can afford the current fares, B) People prefer driving to public transport, C) Lower fares are the main factor affecting ridership, D) Public transportation is safe
- Correct Answer: C) Lower fares are the main factor affecting ridership
- Explanation: The argument assumes that fare cost is a significant barrier to using public transport.

10) **Question:** "More police presence in high-crime areas reduces crime rates because criminals avoid these areas." What assumption is this argument based on?

- Options: A) Criminals fear the police, B) High-crime areas are known, C) Crime can be eliminated, D) There is a shortage of police officers.
- Correct Answer: A) Criminals fear police
- Explanation: The argument assumes that the presence of police deters criminal activity due to fear of apprehension.

11) "All renewable energy sources are environmentally friendly. Solar power is a renewable energy source. Therefore, solar power is environmentally friendly." Is this reasoning valid?

- Options: A) Yes, B) No, C) Only in some cases, D) Cannot determine
- Correct Answer: A) Yes
- Explanation: The argument follows logically, assuming all renewable energy sources, including solar power, are environmentally friendly.

12): "Increasing the tax on cigarettes will reduce smoking because it makes smoking more expensive." What assumption is implicit in this argument?

- Options: A) People will stop smoking entirely, B) Smokers are price-sensitive, C) All smokers want to quit, D) Taxes are the best way to control behavior
- Correct Answer: B) Smokers are price-sensitive
- Explanation: The argument assumes that the cost increase will deter smokers because they are sensitive to price changes.

These sample questions cover a range of critical thinking aspects, such as evaluating arguments, identifying assumptions, and assessing the relevance of information. The correct answers and explanations provided demonstrate the logical processes involved in answering these types of questions accurately.

Types of Reasoning Questions in the OTEE

(C) Problem-Solving Questions

Description

Problem-solving questions assess an individual's ability to apply reasoning skills to solve practical problems. Candidates evaluate scenarios and choose the best course of action. These skills are crucial for CBSA officer trainees in decision-making across various situations.

Examples

1. **Scenario-Based Questions**

   - **Description:** These questions present a detailed scenario and require candidates to choose the best course of action based on the information provided.
   - **Example**: You are a CBSA officer and notice a passenger behaving suspiciously. You must decide whether to question them immediately, observe them for a while longer, or inform your superior.

- **Example:** A shipment has arrived with incomplete documentation. You need to decide whether to hold the shipment for further investigation, release it with a warning, or contact the sender for more information.

2. Situational Judgment Questions

- **Description:** These questions test the ability to prioritize tasks and make decisions under pressure, often presenting multiple options where candidates must select the most appropriate one.
- **Example:** You have several tasks to complete: processing a group of passengers, attending a meeting, and investigating a potential security threat. Which task should you prioritize and why?
- **Example:** A colleague asks for your help with a complex case while you are already handling your workload. How do you manage the situation?

Practice Questions: Scenarios and Problem-Solving Exercises

1) You are a CBSA officer at the airport, and you notice a passenger acting nervously in the customs line. What should you do?

- Options: A) Question the passenger immediately, B) Observe the passenger for a while longer, C) Inform your superior, D) Ignore the passenger
- Correct Answer: B) Observe the passenger for a while longer
- Explanation: Observing the passenger allows you to gather more information and avoid unnecessary confrontation.

2) A shipment of goods arrives with incomplete documentation. What is the best course of action?

- Options: A) Hold the shipment for further investigation, B) Release it with a warning, C) Contact the sender for more information, D) Ignore the missing documentation
- Correct Answer: C) Contact the sender for more information
- Explanation: Contacting the sender can clarify the situation and provide all necessary documentation.

3) Question: You must process a group of passengers, attend a meeting, and investigate a potential security threat. What should you prioritize?

- Options: A) Process the passengers, B) Attend the meeting, C) Investigate the security threat, D) Delegate tasks to colleagues
- Correct Answer: C) Investigate the security threat
- Explanation: A potential security threat is the most urgent and critical task, requiring immediate attention.

4) A colleague asks for your help with a complex case while you are busy with your workload. How do you respond?

- Options: A) Help your colleague immediately, B) Refuse to help, C) Prioritize your work and help later, D) Delegate your tasks to another colleague.
- Correct Answer: C) Prioritize your work and help later
- Explanation: It is important to manage your workload effectively while still being available to assist colleagues when possible.

5) You find a suspicious package in the baggage area. What should you do first?

- Options: A) Open the package to inspect its contents, B) Report it to the security team, C) Move it to a safe area, D) Ignore it
- Correct Answer: B) Report it to the security team
- Explanation: Reporting to the security team ensures that the situation is handled by professionals trained to deal with potential threats.

6) A passenger complains about the long wait time at the border check. How should you handle the situation?

- Options: A) Ignore the complaint, B) Apologize and explain the reason for the delay, C) Speed up the process for that passenger, D) Refer the passenger to a supervisor
- Correct Answer: B) Apologize and explain the reason for the delay
- Explanation: Explaining and showing empathy can help manage the passenger's expectations and reduce frustration.

7) **During a routine check, you discover a passenger with a fake passport. What is the appropriate action?**

- Options: A) Confiscate the passport and let the passenger go, B) Arrest the passenger, C) Report to your superior and follow protocol, D) Ignore it and continue the check.
- Correct Answer: C) Report to your superior and follow protocol
- Explanation: The following protocol ensures that the situation is handled according to CBSA guidelines.

8) **You receive conflicting reports about a security incident. How do you proceed?**

- Options: A) Act immediately on the first report, B) Verify the information before taking action, C) Ignore the reports, and D) Delegate the decision to a colleague.
- Correct Answer: B) Verify the information before taking action
- Explanation: Verifying information ensures you base your actions on accurate and reliable data.

9) **A passenger refuses to comply with a random search. What is your next step?**

- Options: A) Force the search, B) Let the passenger go, C) Explain the importance and seek compliance, D) Call the police
- Correct Answer: C) Explain the importance and seek compliance
- Explanation: Clear communication can help gain the passenger's cooperation without escalating the situation.

10) **You notice a colleague making errors in their documentation. How do you handle this?**

- Options: A) Correct the errors without telling them, B) Report them to a supervisor, C) Offer to help and provide feedback, D) Ignore the errors
- Correct Answer: C) Offer to help and provide feedback
- Explanation: Providing help and constructive feedback can improve accuracy and team performance.

11) A new policy has been implemented, but the team is confused. What should you do?

- Options: A) Ignore the confusion, B) Clarify the policy to the team, C) Wait for a supervisor to address it, D) Continue working as usual
- Correct Answer: B) Clarify the policy to the team
- Explanation: Ensuring everyone understands the new policy can prevent mistakes and improve compliance.

12) A shipment of perishable goods is delayed due to missing paperwork. How do you prioritize handling this situation?

- Options: A) Hold the shipment until the paperwork is complete, B) Expedite the shipment while resolving the paperwork issue, C) Discard the shipment, D) Send the shipment back
- Correct Answer: B) Expedite the shipment while resolving the paperwork issue
- Explanation: Handling the perishable goods quickly can prevent spoilage while addressing the documentation issue.

These sample questions cover a range of problem-solving aspects, such as scenario-based decision-making and situational judgment. The correct answers and explanations provided demonstrate the logical processes involved in answering these types of questions accurately.

Types of Reasoning Questions in the OTEE

(D) Inference Questions

Description

Inference questions assess the ability to draw logical conclusions from given information, which is crucial for CBSA officer trainees to make informed decisions based on limited data.

Examples

1. Drawing Inferences from Given Information

- Description: These questions provide data or a statement and require candidates to determine what can logically be inferred.
- Example: Given a report that states, "The number of border crossings increased by 15% in the last quarter," infer the possible reasons for the increase.
- Example: From a statement like "All officers who received training on the new system reported increased efficiency," infer the relationship between training and efficiency.

2. Identifying Necessary Information for Valid Conclusions

- Description: These questions present a scenario or data set and ask candidates to identify additional information necessary to make a valid conclusion.
- Example: To conclude whether increased patrols reduce illegal crossings, identify what data is necessary beyond the number of patrols and crossing incidents.
- Example: Given the statement "Customer satisfaction improved after implementing a new procedure," determine what additional information is needed to validate this conclusion.

Practice Questions: Exercises to Practice Making Inferences from Information Provided

1) Given the statement, "All imported goods are subject to inspection, and this shipment was inspected," what can be inferred?
- Options: A) This shipment contains imported goods, B) This shipment passed inspection, C) All shipments are inspected, D) This shipment failed inspection
- Correct Answer: A) This shipment contains imported goods
- Explanation: If all imported goods are inspected and this shipment was inspected, it can be inferred that the shipment contains imported goods.

2) The data states that "50% of the seized items were counterfeit electronics." What can be inferred about the rest?

- Options: A) They are all genuine electronics, B) They include non-electronic items, C) They are all counterfeit, D) They are all non-electronic
- Correct Answer: B) They include non-electronic items
- Explanation: Since 50% of the items are counterfeit electronics, the rest must include items other than counterfeit electronics, which could be non-electronic.

3) The report states, "Increased officer training hours correlated with decreased errors." What can be inferred from this statement?

- Options: A) Training causes errors, B) Decreased training leads to fewer errors, C) More training is associated with fewer errors, D) Errors are unrelated to training
- Correct Answer: C) More training is associated with fewer errors
- Explanation: The statement indicates a correlation between increased training hours and decreased errors, suggesting an association.

4) "If the weather is bad, flights are delayed. Today, flights are delayed." What can be inferred?
- Options: A) The weather is bad today, B) All flights are canceled, C) Weather causes delays, D) Cannot determine the cause of the delay
- Correct Answer: D) Cannot determine the cause of the delay
- Explanation: While bad weather can cause delays, there could be other reasons for today's delays. The cause cannot be determined solely based on the given information.

5) Given the data, "Border security incidents decreased by 20% after new measures were implemented," what additional information is necessary to conclude that the new measures caused the decrease?

- Options: A) Comparison with previous incidents, B) Details of the new measures, C) Other factors affecting incidents, D) All of the above
- Correct Answer: D) All of the above
- Explanation: To conclude causation, we need comprehensive data, including comparisons, details of the measures, and other potential influencing factors.

6) The statement reads, "All trainees who completed the advanced course passed the certification exam." What can be inferred about trainees who did not complete the advanced course?

- Options: A) They failed the exam, B) They passed the exam, C) Cannot infer their exam results, D) They did not take the exam.
- Correct Answer: C) Cannot infer their exam results
- Explanation: The statement only provides information about those who completed the course and passed. It does not provide information about those who did not complete the course.

7) "During the holiday season, the number of travelers increases significantly." What can be inferred about border operations during the holiday season?

- Options: A) Operations are the same, B) Increased workload for officers, C) Decrease in operations, D) Border is closed
- Correct Answer: B) Increased workload for officers
- Explanation: An increase in travelers implies more work for border officers.

8) "Illegal crossings are most frequent in the early morning." What can be inferred about the timing of border patrols to maximize effectiveness?

- Options: A) Conduct patrols in the afternoon, B) Increase patrols in the early morning, C) Patrols are not needed, D) Patrols should be randomized
- Correct Answer: B) Increase patrols in the early morning
- Explanation: Increasing patrols during early morning hours would be effective to counter the frequent illegal crossings.

9) "Customer feedback indicates a preference for faster processing times." What can be inferred about customer satisfaction efforts?

- Options: A) Focus on improving facilities, B) Focus on reducing processing times, C) Ignore processing times, D) Increase staffing
- Correct Answer: B) Focus on reducing processing times
- Explanation: Feedback indicates that faster processing times would improve customer satisfaction.

10) Given the statement, "All CBSA officers must pass a background check, and Jane is a CBSA officer," what can be inferred?

- Options: A) Jane has not passed a background check, B) Jane has passed a background check, C) Jane is in training, and D) Jane is exempt from background checks.
- Correct Answer: B) Jane has passed a background check
- Explanation: Since all CBSA officers must pass a background check, and Jane is a CBSA officer, it can be inferred that she has passed the check.

11) "Border security funding increased this year, leading to enhanced surveillance capabilities." What can be inferred about the relationship between funding and surveillance?

- Options: A) Surveillance is independent of funding, B) Funding decreases surveillance, C) Increased funding improves surveillance, D) Surveillance capabilities are reduced
- Correct Answer: C) Increased funding improves surveillance
- Explanation: The statement suggests increased funding has led to better surveillance capabilities.

12) The statement says, "Implementing new technology at border checkpoints reduced wait times by 30%." What can be inferred about the effect of technology on wait times?

- Options: A) Technology increases wait times, B) Technology does not affect wait times, C) New technology reduces wait times, D) Technology is unrelated to wait times
- Correct Answer: C) New technology reduces wait times
- Explanation: The implementation of new technology is associated with a significant reduction in wait times.

These sample questions cover various aspects of making inferences, such as interpreting data, understanding relationships, and identifying necessary information for conclusions. The correct answers and explanations demonstrate the logical processes involved in answering these types of questions accurately.

4. Analytical Thinking

Introduction to Analytical Thinking

Importance of Analytical Thinking for CBSA Officers

Analytical thinking is crucial for Canada Border Services Agency (CBSA) officers, enabling them to accurately assess situations and make informed decisions. This skill is essential for evaluating the risk of individuals and goods entering the country and analyzing data for trends and anomalies.

Definition

Analytical thinking involves using a logical thought process to analyze a situation or problem, systematically examining information, identifying patterns, and drawing logical conclusions.

Relevance

Analytical thinking is applied daily by CBSA officers in several ways:

- **Risk Assessment**: Evaluating the potential threat posed by travelers and shipments.
- **Decision Making**: Making informed decisions based on data and evidence.
- Problem Solving: Identifying issues and determining the best course of action.
- **Data Analysis**: Interpreting data to identify trends and anomalies that could indicate security threats.

Understanding the Types of Analytical Thinking Questions

Analytical thinking questions can be categorized into several types. Each type requires a specific approach and set of skills to solve effectively.

Types of Analytical Thinking Questions

1. **Logical Reasoning**

- These questions assess the ability to analyze arguments and identify logical relationships.
- Example: If all A are B, and all B are C, then all A are C. True or False

2. Pattern Recognition

- Identifying patterns and sequences in data or scenarios.
- Example: What is the next number in the series: 2, 4, 8, 16, ___?

3. Problem Solving

- Involves breaking down complex problems into manageable parts and finding solutions.
- Example: A CBSA officer must decide on resource allocation based on fluctuating passenger volumes at different border points.

4. Data Interpretation

- Analyzing graphs, charts, and tables to conclude.
- Example: Based on the given data table of passenger flow over a week, determine the day with the highest volume.

Strategies to Approach Analytical Problems

1. Break Down the Problem
- Simplify the problem into smaller, more manageable parts.
- Focus on understanding each part before attempting to solve the whole.

2. Identify Patterns
- Look for recurring themes or sequences.
- Use patterns to predict future outcomes or understand the problem's structure.

3. Use Logical Processes
- Apply logical reasoning to connect information and draw conclusions.
- Avoid assumptions and focus on the evidence presented.

4. Practice Regularly
- Consistent practice with various types of questions enhances analytical skills.
- Use sample questions and real-life scenarios for practice.

Practice with Examples and Sample Questions

(A) Logical Reasoning

(1) **All dogs are animals. Some animals are pets. Therefore, all dogs are pets.**

- A. True
- B. False
- C. Cannot be determined
- D. None of the above

Answer: B. False. Not all animals are pets.

(2) **I will go to the beach if it is sunny. It is not sunny. Therefore, I will not go to the beach.**

- A. True
- B. False
- C. Cannot be determined
- D. None of the above

Answer: A. True. The statement follows the initial condition.

(3) **All birds can fly. Penguins are birds. Therefore, all penguins can fly.**

- A. True
- B. False
- C. Cannot be determined
- D. None of the above

Answer: B. False. Penguins are birds but cannot fly.

(4) **If John is taller than Mary, and Mary is taller than Peter, then Peter is taller than John.**

- A. True
- B. False
- C. Cannot be determined
- D. None of the above

Answer: B. False. The information given shows John is the tallest.

(A) Logical Reasoning

(5) No reptiles have fur. Snakes are reptiles. Therefore, snakes have fur.

- A. True
- B. False
- C. Cannot be determined
- D. None of the above

Answer: B. False. The statement contradicts the initial information.

(6) All cars have four wheels. This vehicle has four wheels, so it is a car.

- A. True
- B. False
- C. Cannot be determined
- D. None of the above

Answer: B. False. Other vehicles, like motorcycles with sidecars, can also have four wheels.

(7) If all roses are flowers, and some are red, can we conclude that some roses are red?

- A) Yes
- B) No
- C) Only if all flowers are red
- D) Cannot be determined

Correct Answer: D) Cannot be determined.
Explanation: "Some flowers are red" does not necessarily mean that the subset of roses is red.

(8) What can we conclude if all athletes are fit and all runners are athletes?

- A) All runners are fit
- B) Some runners are fit
- C) No runners are fit
- D) Cannot be determined

Correct Answer: A) All runners are fit
Explanation: Since all athletes are fit and all runners are athletes, it logically follows that all runners are fit.

(A) Logical Reasoning

(9) Which statement is true if some birds can fly, and all parrots are birds?

- A) All parrots can fly
- B) Some parrots cannot fly
- C) Some birds cannot fly
- D) Some parrots can fly

Correct Answer: D) Some parrots can fly.
Explanation: Since parrots are a subset of birds, and some birds can fly, it is possible that some parrots can fly.

(10) If no cats are dogs, and some dogs are pets, can we conclude that some pets are not cats?

- A) Yes
- B) No
- C) Some pets are cats
- D) Cannot be determined

Correct Answer: A) Yes
Explanation: Since no cats are dogs and some dogs are pets, those pets that are dogs are not cats.

(11) If all pens are tools, and some tools are not blue, what can we conclude about pens?

- A) Some pens are blue
- B) No pens are blue
- C) Some pens are not blue
- D) Cannot be determined

Correct Answer: C) Some pens are not blue
Explanation: Since some tools are not blue, and all pens are tools, some pens could also be not blue.

(12) What can we conclude if all fruits are sweet and no lemons are sweet?

- A) All lemons are fruits
- B) No lemons are fruits
- C) Some lemons are fruits
- D) No fruits are lemons

Correct Answer: D) No fruits are lemons
Explanation: Since no lemons are sweet and all fruits are sweet, lemons cannot be fruits.

(B)Pattern Recognition

(1) Identify the next item in the sequence: M2, N3, O4, P5, ___?

- A) Q6
- B) R7
- C) Q5
- D) R6

Correct Answer: A) Q6

Explanation: The pattern involves consecutive letters of the alphabet (M, N, O, P) paired with consecutive numbers (2, 3, 4, 5). The next letter is Q, and the next number is 6.

(2) Identify the next item in the sequence: 5A, 6B, 7C, 8D, ___?

- A) 9E
- B) 10E
- C) 9F
- D) 10F

Correct Answer: A) 9E

Explanation: The pattern involves consecutive numbers (5, 6, 7, 8) paired with letters (A, B, C, D). The next number is 9, and the next letter is E.

(3) Identify the next item in the sequence: Z1, Y2, X3, W4, ___?

- A) V5
- B) U5
- C) V6
- D) U6

Correct Answer: A) V5

Explanation: The pattern involves consecutive letters in reverse order (Z, Y, X, W) paired with consecutive numbers (1, 2, 3, 4). The next letter is V, and the next number is 5.

(4) Identify the next item in the sequence: 2F, 4H, 6J, 8L, ___?

- A) 10N
- B) 10M
- C) 9N
- D) 9M

Correct Answer: A) 10N

Explanation: The pattern involves even numbers increasing by 2 (2, 4, 6, 8) paired with every second letter in the alphabet (F, H, J, L). The next number is 10, and the next letter in the pattern is N.

(B)Pattern Recognition

(5) Identify the next item in the sequence: B3, D5, F7, H9, ___?

- A) J11
- B) I10
- C) J9
- D) K11

Correct Answer: A) J11

Explanation: The pattern involves every second letter of the alphabet (B, D, F, H) paired with consecutive odd numbers increasing by 2 (3, 5, 7, 9). The next letter is J, and the next number is 11.

(6) Identify the next item in the sequence: A10, C8, E6, G4, ___?

- A) I2
- B) J2
- C) H3
- D) I3

Correct Answer: A) I2

Explanation: The pattern involves every second letter of the alphabet (A, C, E, G) paired with even numbers decreasing by 2 (10, 8, 6, 4). The next letter is I, and the next number is 2.

(7)Identify the next item in the sequence: L12, K10, J8, I6, ___?

- A) H4
- B) G4
- C) H5
- D) G5

Correct Answer: A) H4

Explanation: The pattern involves consecutive letters in reverse order (L, K, J, I) paired with even numbers decreasing by 2 (12, 10, 8, 6). The next letter is H, and the next number is 4.

(8) Identify the next item in the sequence: 1M, 2O, 3Q, 4S, ___?

- A) 5U
- B) 5T
- C) 6U
- D) 6T

Correct Answer: A) 5U

Explanation: The pattern involves consecutive numbers (1, 2, 3, 4) paired with every second letter of the alphabet (M, O, Q, S). The next number is 5, and the next letter is U.

(B) Pattern Recognition

(9) Identify the next item in the sequence: 9Z, 7X, 5V, 3T, ___?

- A) 1R
- B) 2R
- C) 1S
- D) 2S

Correct Answer: A) 1R

Explanation: The pattern involves odd numbers decreasing by 2 (9, 7, 5, 3) paired with every second letter in reverse alphabetical order (Z, X, V, T). The next number is 1, and the next letter is R.

(10) Identify the next item in the sequence: 15A, 13C, 11E, 9G, ___?

- A) 7I
- B) 8J
- C) 6H
- D) 7H

Correct Answer: A) 7I

Explanation: The pattern involves odd numbers decreasing by 2 (15, 13, 11, 9) paired with every second letter in the alphabet (A, C, E, G). The next number is 7, and the next letter is I

(11) Identify the next item in the sequence: 14M, 12K, 10I, 8G, ___?

- A) 6E
- B) 5E
- C) 7F
- D) 6F

Correct Answer: A) 6E

Explanation: The pattern involves even numbers decreasing by 2 (14, 12, 10, 8) paired with every second letter in reverse alphabetical order (M, K, I, G). The next number is 6, and the next letter is E.

(12) Identify the next item in the sequence: 4P, 8R, 12T, 16V, ___?

- A) 20X
- B) 20W
- C) 18W
- D) 18X

Correct Answer: A) 20X

Explanation: The pattern involves multiples of 4 increasing by 4 (4, 8, 12, 16) paired with every second letter in the alphabet (P, R, T, V). The next number is 20, and the next letter is X.

Practice with Examples and Sample Questions

(C) Problem-Solving

(1) A CBSA officer has 10 agents and needs to allocate them between two busy border points. If Border Point A requires twice as many agents as Border Point B, how many agents should be allocated to Border Point B?

- A) 2
- B) 3
- C) 4
- D) 5

Correct Answer: C) 4

Let the number of agents at Border Point B be x. Then, Border Point A would require 2x agents. Since there are 10 agents in total, x + 2x = 10. Therefore, 3x = 10, and x = 10/3 = 3.33. Since the number of agents must be a whole number, 4 agents should be allocated to Border Point B and 6 to Border Point A.

(2) The officer has to process 150 passengers in 3 hours at a border checkpoint. If the officer can process 10 passengers in 15 minutes, will the officer complete the task in the given time?

- A) Yes, with time to spare
- B) Yes, just in time
- C) No, the officer will need more time
- D) Not enough information

Answer: C) No, the officer will need more time

The officer can process 10 passengers in 15 minutes, so in 3 hours (180 minutes), the officer can process (180/15) * 10 = 120 passengers. Therefore, the officer can process 120 passengers in 3 hours, so they will need an additional 0.75 hours (45 minutes) to complete the remaining 30 passengers. This means the task will be completed in approximately 3.75 hours, needing more time. The correct answer should be, "No, the officer will need more time."

(3) A CBSA officer must distribute 36 inspection forms equally among 4 desks. How many forms will each desk receive?

- A) 6
- B) 7
- C) 8
- D) 9

Answer: D) 9

The total number of forms is 36, and there are 4 desks. Dividing 36 by 4 gives 36/4 = 9, so each desk will receive 9 forms.

Problem-Solving

(4) At a border checkpoint, there are 5 lanes, and each lane can process 12 vehicles per hour. If the checkpoint is open for 8 hours, what is the maximum number of vehicles that can be processed?

- A) 480
- B) 500
- C) 600
- D) 700

Correct Answer: C) 600
Each lane processes 12 vehicles per hour, and there are 5 lanes, so 12 * 5 = 60 vehicles can be processed in one hour. Over 8 hours, 60 * 8 = 480 vehicles can be processed.

(5) A CBSA officer notices that passenger volume at one checkpoint increases by 20% every hour. If the initial volume is 100 passengers, how many will be at the checkpoint after 2 hours?

- A) 120
- B) 140
- C) 144
- D) 160

Answer: C) 144
After the first hour, the passengers are 100 + (100 * 0.20) = 120. After the second hour, the number of passengers is 120 + (120 * 0.20) = 144.

(6) A border point typically processes 500 passengers per day. Due to an upcoming holiday, passenger volume is expected to increase by 50%. How many passengers should the officer prepare to process on that day?

- A) 650
- B) 700
- C) 750
- D) 800

Answer: C) 750
A 50% increase on 500 passengers is 500 * 0.50 = 250. Therefore, the expected number of passengers is 500 + 250 = 750.

(C) Problem-Solving

(7) A CBSA officer has a budget of $1,000 to allocate among four border checkpoints. If each checkpoint needs an equal share, how much will each checkpoint receive?

- A) $200
- B) $250
- C) $300
- D) $400

Correct Answer: B) $250
The total budget is $1,000, and there are four checkpoints. Dividing $1,000 by 4 gives 1000/4 = 250, and each checkpoint will receive $250.

(8) A CBSA officer can inspect 15 vehicles in 30 minutes. How many vehicles can the officer inspect in 2 hours?

- A) 60
- B) 75
- C) 90
- D) 120

Answer: A) 60
30 Min= 15 vehicle , 30 x4 (120 min = 2 Hr.) = 15x 4 (60 Vehicles)

(9) A border crossing is open 24 hours daily, with 6 agents working each 8-hour shift in a pair simultaneously (3 shifts of 8 hours each, 2 agents working each shift). If the workload increases by 50% in the third shift, how many agents are needed for that shift?

- A) 7
- B) 8
- C) 9
- D)10

Answer: A) 7
A 50% increase in the work of 2 agents in the third shift will add 50% of 2 agents, that is 1 agent. So 2 agent (morning shift) + 2 agents (afternoon shift) + 3 agents (night shift) = 7 agents

(C) Problem-Solving

(10) An officer must divide a shipment of 600 units equally among 5 warehouses. How many units will each warehouse receive?

- A) 100
- B) 120
- C) 140
- D) 150

Correct Answer: B) 120
600 divided by 5 = 120

(11) A checkpoint processes 80 vehicles per hour. How many vehicles should be processed if the officer wants to increase this by 25% in the next hour?

- A) 90
- B) 100
- C) 105
- D) 120

Answer: B) 100

25% of 80= (25/100)x80= 80/4=20 , So 80+ 20 = 100 vehicles

(12) A CBSA officer schedules 4 agents to work 8-hour shifts. If each agent can work up to 40 hours per week, how many shifts can each agent work per week?

- A) 4
- B) 5
- C) 6
- D) 7

Answer: B) 5

40 hours per week / 8 hour shift = 40/8 = 5 shifts

Practice with Examples and Sample Questions

(D) Data Interpretation

(1) The table below shows the number of passengers processed at a border checkpoint over five days. On which day was the highest number of passengers processed?

Day	Passengers
Monday	1,200
Tuesday	1,350
Wednesday	1,100
Thursday	1,450
Friday	1,300

- A) Monday
- B) Tuesday
- C) Thursday
- D) Friday

Correct Answer: C) Thursday
Thursday has the highest number of passengers processed, with 1,450 passengers.

(2) Please review the following data on the number of vehicles processed at three border checkpoints and identify the border checkpoint that shows an inconsistency.

Border Point	Monday	Tuesday	Wednesday	Thursday	Friday
Point A	1,500	1,550	1,600	1,700	1,750
Point B	1,300	1,320	1,350	1,380	1,400
Point C	1,800	1,850	1,900	1,750	1,950

(A) Point A   (B) Point B   (C) Point C   (D) Point D

Correct Answer: C) Thursday
The number of vehicles processed at Point C decreased on Thursday, which is inconsistent with the pattern of gradual increase seen on other days.

(D) Data Interpretation

(3) The table below lists the number of inspections carried out at two border checkpoints over five days. Identify how many discrepancies exist between the two checkpoints.

Day	Checkpoint X	Checkpoint Y
Monday	1,100	1,100
Tuesday	1,250	1,250
Wednesday	1,300	1,310
Thursday	1,450	1,450
Friday	1,500	1,550

- A) 1
- B) 2
- C) 3
- D) 4

Correct Answer: B) 2
Discrepancies are found on Wednesday and Friday, where the number of inspections differs between the two checkpoints.

(4) Analyze the following sequences of vehicle types inspected at two border points and identify the day with a pattern inconsistency.

Day	Border Point X	Border Point Y
Monday	Car	Truck
Tuesday	Truck	Car
Wednesday	Car	Car
Thursday	Truck	car
Friday	Car	Truck

(A) Monday   (B) Tuesday   (C) Wednesday   (D) Friday

Correct Answer: C) Wednesday
 On Wednesday, both border points inspected cars, which is inconsistent with the alternating pattern seen on other days.

(D) Data Interpretation

(5) The table below shows the total number of vehicles inspected at a border checkpoint over a week: What is the total number of vehicles inspected from Monday to Friday?

Day	Vehicles Inspected
Monday	800
Tuesday	950
Wednesday	1,000
Thursday	1,050
Friday	900

- A) 4200 (B) 4700   (C) 3700 (D) None

Correct Answer: (B) 4700
Total Vehicles from Monday to Friday = 800+950+1000+1050+900 =4700

(6) Examine the two lists of security codes used over a day at two border points. Identify how many discrepancies are found between them.

Border Point 1:
B50012, H75093, L29018, T48920, Q00123

Border Point 2:
B50012, H75093, L29018, T48920, Q00132

Question: How many discrepancies exist between the lists?

- A) 0
- B) 1
- C) 2
- D) 3

Correct Answer: B) 1

Explanation: The discrepancy is in the last code, where the sequence "Q00132" at Border Point 2 differs from "Q00123" at Border Point 1.

(D) Data Interpretation

(7) The table below shows the percentage distribution of vehicle types inspected at a border checkpoint. What percentage of the vehicles inspected were Trucks or Buses?

Vehicle Type	Percentage
Cars	40%
Trucks	35%
Buses	15%
Motorcycles	10%

- A) 40% (B) 50% (C) 55% (D) None

Correct Answer: (B) 50%

35(Truck) + 15 (Buses) = 50%

(8) The line graph below shows the weekly passenger volume at a checkpoint over five weeks: In which week did the checkpoint see the greatest increase in passenger volume compared to the previous week?

- A) Week 2
- B) Week 3
- C) Week 4
- D) Week 5

Correct Answer: A) Week 2

Explanation: The greatest increase occurred between Week 1 and Week 2, with an increase of 1,200–1,000=2001,200 - 1,000 = 2001,200–1,000=200 passengers.

(D) Data Interpretation

(9) Review the following two lists of identification codes from a border checkpoint and determine how many discrepancies are between them. How many discrepancies are there between the lists?

List 1:
KJ23481, LM39475, NP50621, QW73819, TR48902
List 2:
KJ23481, LM39475, NP50612, QW73819, TR48902

- A) 1
- B) 2
- C) 3
- D) 4

- **Correct Answer:** A) 1
- **Explanation:** The discrepancy is in the third code, where "NP50621" from List 1 is written as "NP50612" in List 2.

(10) Border Point X:

G56012, B49085, C20391, D67104, E38420
Border Point Y:
G56012, B49085, C20391, D67104, E38402

Question: How many discrepancies are between the records of Border Point X and Border Point Y?

- A) 0
- B) 1
- C) 2
- D) 3

Correct Answer: B) 1
Explanation: The last code "E38402" in Border Point Y differs from "E38420" in Border Point X, making it the only discrepancy between the two records.

(D) Data Interpretation

(11) The bar graph below shows the number of passengers processed at two different border points during the peak hours of the day. How many more passengers were processed at Point B compared to Point A?

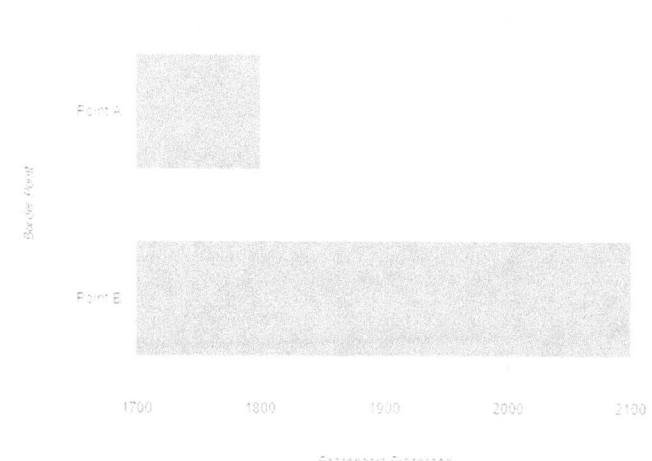

- A) 200
- B) 300
- C) 400
- D) 500

- **Correct Answer:** B) 300
- **Explanation:** Point B processed 300 more passengers than Point A: 2100−1800=300

(12) Analyze the following data on passenger volumes over five days at two border points and identify the day with a discrepancy.

Day	Border Point A	Border Point B
Monday	800	750
Tuesday	850	800
Wednesday	900	850
Thursday	950	900
Friday	1,000	870

- A) Monday
- B) Tuesday
- C) Thursday
- D) Friday

Correct Answer: D) Friday
- **Explanation:** The number of passengers at Border Point B decreases on Friday, inconsistent with the increase at Border Point A and the general trend.

5. Client service orientation

Importance of Client Service Orientation for CBSA Officers

Overview

Client service orientation means providing the best possible service to internal and external clients. This includes ensuring quality, timeliness, completeness, knowledge, competence, courtesy, fairness, and positive outcomes. For CBSA officers, this involves delivering exceptional service while upholding the agency's standards and regulations.

Relevance

Client service orientation plays a vital role in the daily operations and decision-making processes of CBSA officers. Here's how it applies:

- Interaction with the Public: CBSA officers are responsible for ensuring travelers have a smooth experience while entering the country. This involves providing accurate information, addressing concerns promptly, and resolving issues efficiently.
- Internal Collaboration: Officers frequently collaborate with other units within the agency. To maintain high service standards, it is essential to provide clear, constructive feedback and ensure that internal communications are effective and courteous.
- Problem Resolution: When errors or issues arise, officers must take the initiative to correct them while maintaining a positive and professional demeanor.

Understanding the Types of Client Service Orientation Questions

Client service orientation questions typically assess an officer's ability to respond to various scenarios in a way that balances service quality with regulatory enforcement. These questions may include:

1) Scenario-Based Questions

- These questions present hypothetical situations where the officer must choose the most appropriate action to provide the best service.

- **Example**: You are called upon to review a report from another unit and notice inconsistencies in the data. What is the most effective way to address this?

2) Prioritization and Decision Making

- Assess an officer's ability to prioritize tasks and make decisions that benefit clients and the agency.
- **Example:** How would you prioritize assistance for multiple travelers simultaneously?

3) Communication and Feedback

- These questions evaluate the officer's ability to communicate clearly and provide constructive feedback.
- **Example:** After reviewing a report, you find errors. How do you communicate this to the team that created it?

Strategies to Approach Client Service Orientation Problems

Deliver Quality Service

- Focus on providing complete and accurate information to clients.
- Ensure that all interactions are timely, courteous, and fair.

Handle Issues with Professionalism

- When encountering errors or problems, take corrective action while maintaining a professional tone.
- Provide constructive feedback that encourages improvement without undermining the efforts of others.

Communicate Effectively

- Use clear, straightforward language to convey information and feedback.
- Always aim for a solution that balances the client's needs with the agency's requirements.

Prioritize and Make Decisions Wisely

- Prioritize tasks based on urgency and importance.
- Make decisions ensuring the best possible outcomes for the client and the agency.

Practice with Examples and Sample Questions
(A) Scenario-Based Question

(1) You are working at a busy border crossing, and a traveler is upset because their luggage has been misplaced. They are raising their voice and demanding immediate assistance. What is the most effective way to handle the situation?

- a) Calmly explain that you are doing your best and ask them to wait patiently.
- b) Ignore the traveler and focus on the next person in line.
- c) Raise your voice to match theirs and tell them to calm down.
- d) Acknowledge their frustration, assure them you will help, and immediately start locating their luggage.

Correct Answer: d) Acknowledge their frustration, assure them you will help, and immediately start locating their luggage.
Explanation: This option shows empathy, takes control of the situation, and initiates a solution, which are key elements of client service orientation.

(2) A colleague has asked you to review their prepared document. You find several minor errors that need correction. What is the best course of action?

- a) Make the corrections yourself and return the document without comment.
- b) Point out the errors in a detailed email and ask your colleague to fix them.
- c) Make the corrections and explain to your colleague what was wrong and how to avoid such errors in the future.
- d) Ignore the errors and submit the document as is.

Correct Answer: c) Make the corrections and explain to your colleague what was wrong and how to avoid such errors in the future.
Explanation: This approach not only corrects mistakes but also helps your colleague improve, which is a positive and constructive approach.

(3) You are managing a line of travelers at a checkpoint when one traveler begins to argue with another over the order in the queue. What should you do?

a) Tell them to settle it themselves and continue processing the next traveler.
b) Ignore the argument and focus on your tasks.
c) Step in, separate the travelers, and, based on the facts, determine who should be next in line.
d) Call security to handle the situation.

Correct Answer: c) Step in, separate the travelers, and determine who should be next in line based on the facts.
Explanation: This option ensures the situation is managed fairly and promptly, reducing tension and maintaining order.

(A) Scenario-Based Question

(4) A traveler seems frustrated and worried about why they must declare certain items. How should you respond?

- a) Provide a printed brochure and ask them to read it independently.
- b) Briefly explain the process and move on to the next traveler.
- c) Thoroughly explain the declaration process in simple terms, answering any questions they have.
- d) Ignore their concerns and focus on processing their paperwork.

Correct Answer: c) Thoroughly explain the declaration process in simple terms, answering any questions they have.
Explanation: Providing clear information in a patient manner ensures the traveler understands the rules and feels supported.

(5) During a routine inspection, you discover that a traveler has inadvertently failed to declare a prohibited item. What is the best course of action?

- a) Immediately confiscate the item and impose a fine.
- b) Politely explain the issue to the traveler, confiscate the item, and provide information on why it is prohibited.
- c) Let the traveler go without consequences since it was an honest mistake.
- d) Detain the traveler for further questioning.

Correct Answer: b) Politely explain the issue to the traveler, confiscate the item, and provide information on why it is prohibited.
Explanation: This response ensures the law is enforced while educating the traveler to prevent future mistakes.

(6) You are reviewing a report from another unit and find that the data is inconsistent. What should you do first?

- a) Submit the report as is and note the inconsistencies in your feedback.
- b) Compare the data to other reports to verify the inconsistencies.
- c) Contact the unit that created the report and ask for clarification on the data.
- d) Correct the inconsistencies yourself and finalize the report.

Correct Answer: c) Contact the unit that created the report and ask for clarification on the data.
Explanation: It's important to clarify the issue with the original creators to ensure accuracy and maintain collaborative relationships.

(A) Scenario-Based Question

(7) A traveler with a disability is struggling to complete the required customs declaration forms. What should you do?

- a) Assist the traveler in completing the forms, ensuring they understand each section.
- b) Tell them to do their best and complete the rest later.
- c) Complete the forms for them without asking questions.
- d) Direct them to another officer for assistance.

Correct Answer: a) Assist the traveler in completing the forms, ensuring they understand each section.
Explanation: Offering direct and clear assistance ensures that the traveler's needs are met and the process is completed correctly.

(8) You are working with a new colleague struggling to keep up with the pace at the checkpoint. What is the most effective way to support them?

- a) Offer to help them with their tasks and provide tips on improving efficiency.
- b) Ignore the situation and focus on your work.
- c) Report them to your supervisor for being too slow.
- d) Take over their tasks completely to speed things up.

Correct Answer: a) Offer to help them with their tasks and provide tips on improving efficiency.
Explanation: This approach supports your colleague's development and helps maintain a smooth workflow.

(9) A frequent traveler has approached you with a complaint about a rule they find inconvenient. How should you handle the situation?

- a) Explain the rule and why it is necessary, listening to their concerns.
- b) Apologize and tell them you will look into changing the rule.
- c) Ignore the complaint and continue processing other travelers.
- d) Tell the traveler that the rule cannot be changed and that they must follow it.

Correct Answer: a) Explain the rule clearly and why it is necessary, listening to their concerns.
Explanation: This approach provides the traveler with an understanding of the rule while acknowledging their concerns.

(A) Scenario-Based Question

(10) While processing a family, you notice that one of the children appears ill and their paperwork is incomplete. What should you do?

- a) Complete the paperwork for them and let them through.
- b) Process the family but advise them to see a doctor.
- c) Pause the process, ensure the paperwork is completed correctly, and suggest they seek medical attention.
- d) Deny entry until the paperwork is fully completed.

Correct Answer: c) Pause the process, ensure the paperwork is completed correctly, and suggest they seek medical attention.
Explanation: This option ensures that all legal requirements are met while showing concern for the family's well-being.

(11) A traveler accidentally leaves a valuable item at your station. What is the most appropriate action?

- a) Keep the item safe and attempt to contact the traveler.
- b) Leave the item where it was found and continue working.
- c) Take the item to lost and found and forget about it.
- d) Hold onto the item until the traveler returns looking for it.

Correct Answer: a) Keep the item safe and attempt to contact the traveler.
Explanation: This ensures the traveler's property is secure and shows high client service.

(12) You are in charge of a busy checkpoint and notice that the lines are growing long, causing frustration among travelers. What is the best way to address the situation?

- a) Apologize to the travelers and continue at your current pace.
- b) Call additional staff to help manage the lines and explain the delay to the travelers.
- c) Ignore the situation and focus on processing travelers as quickly as possible.
- d) Ask travelers to be patient without taking further action.

Correct Answer: b) Call additional staff to help manage the lines and explain the delay to the travelers.
Explanation: This option addresses the immediate issue by increasing staff support and communicating with travelers to reduce frustration.

Practice with Examples and Sample Questions
(B) Prioritization and Decision Making

(1) You are managing a busy checkpoint when you receive a call about a suspicious package in the baggage area. At the same time, a traveler approaches you, needing urgent assistance with their paperwork. What should you prioritize?

- a) Address the traveler's paperwork immediately and deal with the suspicious package afterward.
- b) Inform the traveler that you'll return shortly and investigate the suspicious package first.
- c) Ask a colleague to handle the traveler's paperwork while you check on the suspicious package.
- d) Ignore the call about the suspicious package and focus on helping the traveler.

Correct Answer: c) Ask a colleague to handle the traveler's paperwork while you check on the suspicious package.
Explanation: This option ensures that the potential security threat is addressed promptly while the traveler's needs are still met.

(2) Several travelers arrive at your checkpoint simultaneously: one is a VIP, another is a family with young children, and the third is a person with a disability. How should you prioritize processing them?

- a) Process the VIP first, followed by the family, then the person with a disability.
- b) Process the person with a disability first, followed by the family, then the VIP.
- c) Process the family first, followed by the VIP, then the person with a disability.
- d) Process them in the order they arrived, without prioritizing them.

Correct Answer: b) Process the person with a disability first, followed by the family, then the VIP.
Explanation: This option prioritizes based on immediate needs and accessibility, which aligns with good client service and ethical decision-making.

(3) You are finalizing an important report due by the end of the day, but a traveler has just reported a lost item. What should you do?

a) Pause work on the report to help the traveler find their lost item.
b) Continue working on the report and address the traveler's issue later.
c) Delegate helping the traveler to a colleague while you finish the report.
d) Ignore the traveler's issue and focus on completing the report.

Correct Answer: c) Delegate the task of helping the traveler to a colleague while you finish the report.
Explanation: Delegating ensures that both the urgent task and the traveler's needs are addressed without compromising either.

(B) Prioritization and Decision Making

(4) You oversee travelers' processing when you receive an alert about a potential security threat at another checkpoint. What is your priority?

- a) Continue processing travelers at your checkpoint and ignore the alert.
- b) Alert your supervisor and request guidance on how to proceed.
- c) Immediately leave your post to investigate the threat.
- d) Stop processing travelers and focus on the alert, without informing anyone.

Correct Answer: b) Alert your supervisor and request guidance on proceeding.
Explanation: This option ensures the chain of command is followed, and the appropriate response is coordinated.

(5) You are responsible for supervising a team when you notice one of your team members is struggling with their tasks. At the same time, you receive a time-sensitive request from your supervisor. What should you prioritize?

- a) Assist your struggling team member first, then address your supervisor's request.
- b) Focus on completing your supervisor's request and let your team member manage independently.
- c) Delegate your supervisor's request to another team member and help the struggling one.
- d) Complete your supervisor's request first, then assist your team member.

Correct Answer: d) Complete your supervisor's request first, then assist your team member.
Explanation: Meeting the supervisor's request is a priority, but assistance to the team member should follow immediately after to ensure continued team productivity.

(6) While on duty, you receive two requests: one from a colleague needing urgent assistance with a traveler and another from a supervisor asking for a report update. What do you do?

a) Help your colleague first, then update the report.
b) Update the report first, then assist your colleague.
c) Tell your colleagues to handle the situation and focus on the report.
d) Ask another colleague to update the report while you assist with the traveler.

Correct Answer: a) Help your colleague first, then update the report.
Explanation: Assisting with an urgent traveler situation takes immediate priority, but the report update should follow as soon as possible.

(B) Prioritization and Decision Making

(7) You are processing travelers when you notice one who appears anxious and confused. Simultaneously, a supervisor asks for a quick meeting. What should you do?

- a) Attend the meeting with your supervisor first and deal with the traveler afterward.
- b) Assist the traveler immediately and inform your supervisor that you will attend the meeting shortly.
- c) Ask a colleague to assist the traveler while you attend the meeting.
- d) Ignore the traveler's behavior and attend the meeting.

Correct Answer: b) Assist the traveler immediately and inform your supervisor that you will attend the meeting shortly.
Explanation: Prioritizing the traveler's immediate needs shows good client service, but communicating with your supervisor ensures they understand the brief delay.

(8) A traveler has left a piece of luggage unattended; simultaneously, a family is requesting assistance completing their paperwork. What should you prioritize?

- a) Assist the family first, then check on the unattended luggage.
- b) Check on the unattended luggage immediately, then assist the family.
- c) Delegate the luggage issue to a colleague and help the family.
- d) Ignore the luggage and help the family with their paperwork.

Correct Answer: b) Check on the unattended luggage immediately, then assist the family.
Explanation: Unattended luggage poses a potential security threat, which must be addressed immediately to ensure safety.

(9) You review documents when notified that a traveler with a medical emergency needs immediate attention. However, you are almost finished with the documents that are due soon. What should you do?

a) Complete the document review first, then address the medical emergency.
b) Pause the document review and attend to the medical emergency immediately.
c) Ignore the medical emergency and focus on finishing the documents.
d) Ask a colleague to handle the medical emergency while you finish the documents.

Correct Answer: b) Pause the document review and attend to the medical emergency immediately.
Explanation: A medical emergency is a high-priority situation requiring immediate document review attention.

(B) Prioritization and Decision Making

(10) During a busy period, you receive multiple requests: one from a colleague needing help with a difficult traveler, another from a supervisor for an immediate report update, and a third from a traveler who needs assistance. What should you prioritize?

- a) Assist your colleague with the difficult traveler, then handle the report update.
- b) Update the report for your supervisor, then assist your colleague.
- c) Help the traveler first, update the report, and assist your colleague afterward.
- d) Ignore all the requests and focus on processing travelers.

Correct Answer:c) Help the traveler first, update the report, and assist your colleague afterward.
Explanation: Prioritize the traveler's immediate needs, followed by the time-sensitive report update, and then help your colleague.

(11) You are managing a line of travelers when a traveler with a disability arrives needing assistance. At the same time, a supervisor asks for a quick update on a project. How should you prioritize?

- a) Assist the traveler with a disability, then give your supervisor the update.
- b) Give your supervisor the update first, then assist the traveler with a disability.
- c) Ask another officer to assist the traveler while you update your supervisor.
- d) Ignore the traveler's needs and focus on your supervisor's request.

Correct Answer: a) Assist the traveler with a disability, then give your supervisor the update.
Explanation: Assisting the traveler first ensures immediate client service, while the supervisor's update can be provided shortly after.

(12) You are about to finalize a report when you notice a new colleague struggling with an urgent task. What should you do?

a) Finalize your report first, then assist your colleague.
b) Stop working on your report and help your colleague immediately.
c) Delegate the task to another colleague and continue with your report.
d) Ignore your colleague's struggle and focus on completing the report.

Correct Answer: a) Finalize your report first, then assist your colleague.
Explanation: Completing the report ensures that you meet your responsibilities, and you can still provide assistance afterward to support your colleague.

Practice with Examples and Sample Questions
(C) Communication Skills

(1) A traveler approaches you with limited English skills and is confused about the customs declaration process. What is the best way to communicate with them?

- a) Speak slowly and loudly in English, repeating the instructions several times.
- b) Provide a written pamphlet and direct them to read it.
- c) Use simple language and visual aids to explain the process clearly.
- d) Tell them to come back when they can communicate better.

Correct Answer: c) Use simple language and visual aids to explain the process clearly.
Explanation: Using simple language and visual aids helps ensure the traveler understands, even if their English proficiency is limited. It's a clear and empathetic approach.

(2) You are explaining a complicated customs regulation to a traveler who is becoming increasingly frustrated. What is the best way to handle this situation?

- a) Continue explaining in detail, ignoring the traveler's frustration.
- b) Ask the traveler to calm down and listen carefully to your explanation.
- c) Acknowledge the traveler's frustration and offer to explain it in simpler terms.
- d) Suggest that the traveler read the information on their own.

Correct Answer: c) Acknowledge the traveler's frustration and offer to explain it in simpler terms.
Explanation: Acknowledging frustration shows empathy, and offering a simpler explanation helps reduce the traveler's confusion and stress.

(3) A traveler has difficulty understanding why they must pay a duty on certain goods. How should you explain it to them?

a) Briefly state that the law requires it and move on.
b) Explain the specific regulations clearly and relate them to the traveler's situation.
c) Direct them to the website to read the regulations themselves.
d) Tell them that paying the duty is non-negotiable, and they should not argue.

Correct Answer: b) Explain the specific regulations clearly and relate them to the traveler's situation.
Explanation: Relating the regulation to the traveler's situation helps clarify the necessity of the duty and maintains a helpful, informative tone.

(C) Communication Skills

(4) A colleague has misunderstood an important procedural update, and their actions could cause delays at the border. How do you communicate this to them?

- a) Criticize them in front of the team for not understanding the update.
- b) Send them an email explaining what they did wrong.
- c) Talk to them privately, clarify the update, and offer support if needed.
- d) Ignore it and hope they figure it out on their own.

Correct Answer c) Talk to them privately, clarify the update, and offer support if needed.
Explanation: Addressing the issue privately and offering support ensures effective communication while maintaining professionalism and teamwork.

(5) You notice a group of travelers at your checkpoint looking confused about the queue system. How do you address this?

- a) Use the loudspeaker to tell them to get in line.
- b) Could you approach them and explain how the queue system works?
- c) Wait for them to figure it out themselves.
- d) Direct them to the information desk.

Correct Answer:b) You can approach them and explain how the queue system works.
Explanation: Approaching the travelers and explaining the process personally ensures they understand and creates a positive experience at the border.

(6) A traveler seems upset after being selected for additional screening. How do you handle their concerns?

a) Ignore their emotions and focus on the procedure.
b) Tell them nothing to be upset about and continue the process.
c) Acknowledge their concern and calmly explain the reason for the additional screening.
d) Reassure them it's just standard procedure and continue without explanation.

Correct Answer: c) Acknowledge their concern and explain the reason for the additional screening calmly.
Explanation: Acknowledging the traveler's emotions and calmly explaining the process reduces anxiety and builds trust in the system.

(C) Communication Skills

(7) A traveler does not understand the immigration form and asks you for assistance. How do you respond?

- a) Provide them with a copy of the form's instructions and move on.
- b) Give them a brief, generic explanation.
- c) Explain the form in detail, patiently guiding them through each section.
- d) Direct them to another officer for assistance.

Correct Answer c) Explain the form in detail, guiding them through each section patiently.
Explanation: Taking the time to guide the traveler through the form ensures they complete it correctly and provides excellent client service.

(8) You assist one traveler when another interrupts and asks a question. What is the best response?

- a) Tell the second traveler to wait until you're finished.
- b) Ask the second traveler to be patient and that you will assist them shortly.
- c) Answer the second traveler's question quickly, then continue with the first.
- d) Ignore the second traveler and focus on the task at hand.

Correct Answer: b) Ask the second traveler to be patient and that you will assist them shortly.
Explanation: This approach acknowledges the second traveler without interrupting your current task, ensuring both travelers are helped efficiently.

(9) A traveler does not agree with your decision regarding their customs declaration. How do you communicate your decision?

a) Stick to your decision without explaining it further.
b) Explain the reasoning behind your decision, using clear and factual language.
c) Apologize and change your decision to avoid confrontation.
d) Direct them to your supervisor for further explanation.

Correct Answer: b) Explain the reasoning behind your decision, using clear and factual language.
Explanation: Providing a clear and factual explanation of your decision helps the traveler understand the reasoning and reduces the potential for conflict.

(C) Communication Skills

(10) A traveler asks a question about a process you are unfamiliar with. How do you respond?

- a) Guess the answer based on your best judgment.
- b) Tell them you don't know and direct them to another officer.
- c) Inform them that you will find out and get back to them with accurate information.
- d) Ignore their question and move on.

Correct Answer c) Inform them you will find out and get back to them with accurate information.
Explanation: Admitting uncertainty and promising accurate information demonstrates professionalism and ensures the traveler receives correct details.

(11) You explain a complex regulation to travelers, but they seem confused. What is the best approach?

- a) Continue explaining until they understand.
- b) Ask if they have specific questions and break the regulation down into simpler terms.
- c) Give them written information to read on their own.
- d) Refer to the website for more details.

Correct Answer: b) Ask if they have specific questions and break the regulation down into simpler terms.
Explanation: Asking questions and simplifying complex information shows that you are attentive to the traveler's needs and improves their understanding.

(12) You are training a new officer struggling to communicate effectively with travelers. How do you provide feedback?

- a) Publicly point out their mistakes to ensure they learn quickly.
- b) Ignore their mistakes and let them learn on their own.
- c) Give them private, constructive feedback, offering suggestions for improvement.
- d) Send them an email listing all their communication errors.

Correct Answer: c) Give them private, constructive feedback, offering suggestions for improvement.
Explanation: Providing private, constructive feedback supports the new officer's growth and ensures they improve without feeling embarrassed or discouraged.

6. Writing Skills

Introduction to Writing Skills

Practical writing skills are essential for CBSA officers because their responsibilities include documenting interactions, creating reports, and maintaining clear, professional communication. Strong writing skills ensure that important details are accurately conveyed, making processes smoother and decisions well-documented.

Overview

Definition:

Writing skills encompass the capacity to clearly and effectively convey information through written communication. For CBSA officers, this includes composing reports, drafting memos, and completing documentation with precision and clarity.

Relevance:

CBSA officers require strong writing skills as they regularly document incidents, file reports, and maintain records. Poorly written reports can cause misunderstandings, delays, and legal issues.

Why Writing Skills Are Important for CBSA Officers:

Accurate Documentation:

CBSA officers are required to document interactions with travelers, offer written explanations for decisions, and elaborate on observations. Using clear and concise language is crucial to ensure these documents are easily understandable.

Decision-Making Support:

Proper documentation enables officers to make informed decisions based on past interactions and recorded incidents. Your written reports, which often serve as references during investigations, audits, or legal proceedings, are crucial to ensuring a secure and confident decision-making process.

Client Service and Public Trust:

Communicating effectively in writing encourages transparency.

For example, when travelers request written explanations of decisions or policies, CBSA officers must provide concise, clear, and professional responses.

Types of Writing Skills Questions

Writing skills questions can evaluate different aspects of written communication, such as clarity, grammar, organization, and the ability to convey complex information succinctly. Here are the primary types of questions you may encounter:

- **Grammar and Syntax**: This course focuses on the correct use of language, including sentence structure, punctuation, and spelling.
- **Clarity and Precision**: Ensures the message is easy to understand and free of unnecessary jargon or ambiguity.
- **Report Writing**: Tests your ability to organize thoughts, summarize incidents, and convey critical information in a structured manner.

Approach to Solving Writing Skills Questions

- **Read Carefully**: Always read the prompt and guidelines for the question carefully before beginning your response.
- **Plan Your Response**: For more extended responses, such as writing a memo or report, could you outline your main points before starting to write? This helps to organize thoughts and ensure that all relevant information is included.
- **Be Clear and Concise:** Avoid unnecessary words and jargon. Keep sentences short and to the point to ensure clarity.
- **Proofread**: Always check your writing for grammar and punctuation errors before submitting your response.

Example 1: Completing a Report

Scenario:
A traveler arriving from a non-exempt country fails to declare agricultural goods, and you, as the CBSA officer, must document the situation in a report.

Sample Report:

Writing skills questions can evaluate different aspects of written communication, such as clarity, grammar, organization, and the ability to convey complex information succinctly. Here are the primary types of questions you may encounter:

- **Grammar and Syntax**: This course focuses on the correct use of language, including sentence structure, punctuation, and spelling.
- **Clarity and Precision**: Ensures the message is easy to understand and free of unnecessary jargon or ambiguity.
- **Report Writing**: Tests your ability to organize thoughts, summarize incidents, and convey critical information in a structured manner.

Approach to Solving Writing Skills Questions

- **Read Carefully**: Always read the prompt and guidelines for the question carefully before beginning your response.
- **Plan Your Response**: For more extended responses, such as writing a memo or report, could you outline your main points before starting to write? This helps to organize thoughts and ensure that all relevant information is included.
- **Be Clear and Concise:** Avoid unnecessary words and jargon. Keep sentences short and to the point to ensure clarity.
- **Proofread**: Always check your writing for grammar and punctuation errors before submitting your response.

Example 1: Completing a Report

Scenario:
A traveler arriving from a non-exempt country fails to declare agricultural goods, and you, as the CBSA officer, must document the situation in a report.

Traveler Information	Incident Details	Outcome
Name: John Doe	Failed to declare fruits and vegetables.	Traveler received a warning.
Passport No.: XXXXXXXX	Inspected baggage, found undeclared goods.	Goods confiscated, no fine.
Nationality: Canadian	Non-exempt country, agricultural goods.	Documented for future reference.

Writing Task:

Write a summary report based on the scenario.

Answer Example:

"Upon inspection, traveler John Doe, arriving from a non-exempt country, was found with undeclared agricultural goods. The traveler was warned, and the goods were confiscated per CBSA regulations. A detailed report has been filed for future reference."

Example 2: Writing a Decision Explanation

Scenario:

You have been denied entry as a traveler due to incomplete visa documentation. The traveler asks for a written explanation for your decision.

Task:
Could you draft a formal response to the traveler explaining your decision?

Answer Example:

DearJohn,

After reviewing your documents, we determined that your visa requirements still need to be completed as per current entry regulations. Unfortunately, the appropriate documentation cannot permit entry into the country. We'd like to encourage you to obtain the necessary visa and reapply for entry. Should you have any questions, please do not hesitate to contact us.

Sincerely,
Maddy R.
CBSA Officer

Practice with Examples and Sample Questions
(A) Sentence Structure and Word Arrangement

(1) First, arrange the following words to form a complete sentence:
report will the filed be officer by after investigation the
Second, from the choices below, please select the response option that includes the first letter of the second word followed by the last letter of the last word of the sentence.

- a) R N
- b) W N
- c) B E
- d) T N

Correct Answer: A) RN
Explanation: The correct sentence is: "The report will be filed by the officer after the investigation." The second word is "report" (R), and the last word is "investigation" (N).

(2) First, arrange the following words to form a complete sentence:
must all declared goods be properly
Second, from the choices below, please select the response option that includes the first letter of the second word followed by the last letter of the last word of the sentence.

- a) A Y
- b) M T
- c) G Y
- d) GD

Correct Answer: d) GD
Explanation: The correct sentence is: "All goods must be properly declared." The second word is "goods" (G), and the last word is "declared" (D).

(3) First, arrange the following words to form a complete sentence:
officer completed the after the was documentation thoroughly checked
Second, from the choices below, please select the response option that includes the fifth letter of the second word followed by the fifth letter of the last word of the sentence.

a) C K
b) D E
c) O D
d) T D

Correct Answer: a) C K
Explanation: The correct sentence is: "The officer completed the documentation after it was thoroughly checked." The second word is "officer" (C), and the last word is "checked" (K).

(A) Sentence Structure and Word Arrangement

(4) First, arrange the following words to form a complete sentence:
filed records will be kept for review

Second, from the choices below, please select the response option that includes the first letter of the third word followed by the last letter of the last word of the sentence.

- a) F W
- b) R Y
- c) W E
- d) B W

Correct Answer: d) B W

Explanation: The correct sentence is: "Records will **b**e filed and kept for revie**w**."

(5) First, arrange the following words to form a complete sentence:
passport submitted after must documentation be the review

Second, from the choices below, please select the response option that includes the first letter of the third word followed by the last letter of the last word of the sentence.

- a) P W
- b) M W
- c) D E
- d) A T

Correct Answer: b) M W

Explanation: The correct sentence is: "The passport **m**ust be submitted after the documentation revie**w**.

6) Arrange the following words to form a complete sentence: *document correctly must signed be the by applicant*

- a) The document must be signed by the applicant correctly.
- b) The document must correctly be signed by the applicant.
- c) The applicant must correctly sign the document.
- d) The document must be correctly signed by the applicant.

Correct Answer:
d) The document must be correctly signed by the applicant.

Explanation:
This arrangement provides the most clear and logical sentence, placing the subject ("document") first, followed by the action ("signed") and the performer of the action ("applicant").

Practice with Examples and Sample Questions
(B) Grammar and Syntax

(1) Which of the following sentences is grammatically correct?

- a) The officers was ready for their assignments.
- b) The officers were ready for their assignments.
- c) The officers is ready for their assignments.
- d) The officers are ready for his assignment.

Correct Answer: b) The officers were ready for their assignments.
Explanation: The subject "officers" is plural, so the verb must be "were," not "was" or "is," and "assignments" must match the plural subject.

(2) Choose the correct sentence:

- a) The report that the officer reviewed, it was incomplete.
- b) The report which the officer reviewed was incomplete.
- c) The report that the officer reviewed was incomplete.
- d) The report, which the officer reviewed, it was incomplete.

Correct Answer: c) The report that the officer reviewed was incomplete.
Explanation: Option (c) correctly uses "that" as a restrictive relative pronoun to link "report" to the description "the officer reviewed."

(3) Which sentence is correctly punctuated?

a) The officer, quickly checked the document and, handed it back.
b) The officer quickly checked the document and handed it back.
c) The officer, quickly checked, the document and handed it back.
d) The officer quickly, checked the document, and handed it back.

Correct Answer: b) The officer quickly checked the document and handed it back.
Explanation: Option (b) correctly avoids unnecessary commas and maintains proper sentence flow.

4) Identify the grammatically correct sentence:

- a) The officers has completed their training last week.
- b) The officers completed their training last week.
- c) The officers were completing their training last week.
- d) The officers will completed their training last week.

Correct Answer: b) The officers completed their training last week.
Explanation: The past tense "completed" is correct for describing an action finished in the past, making option (b) the correct choice.

Practice with Examples and Sample Questions
(C) Clarity and Precision

(1) Which sentence is the clearest and most precise?

- a) The officer checked the document to see if there were any mistakes in it.
- b) The officer checked to ensure that the document was free from errors.
- c) The officer carefully looked over the document for possible mistakes.
- d) The officer reviewed the document with caution to avoid any potential errors.

Correct Answer: b) The officer checked to ensure that the document was free from errors.
Explanation: Option (b) is concise and specific, avoiding unnecessary words and clearly expressing the action with "checked" and "free from errors."

(2) Choose the sentence that most clearly conveys the officer's action:

- a) The officer started to write the report at the end of the shift.
- b) The officer began drafting the report towards the end of the shift.
- c) The officer began composing the report after his shift had nearly ended.
- d) The officer worked on writing the report as his shift was finishing.

Correct Answer: b) The officer began drafting the report towards the end of the shift.
Explanation: Option (b) is the clearest, using "drafting" to specify the writing process and directly stating when the action occurred.

(3) Which sentence is most precise?

a) The officer made sure that the traveler understood the procedure.
b) The officer ensured that the traveler comprehended the procedure clearly.
c) The officer confirmed that the traveler fully understood the procedure.
d) The officer checked to see if the traveler got what he needed to do.

Correct Answer: c) The officer confirmed that the traveler fully understood the procedure.
Explanation: Option (c) is both clear and precise, using "confirmed" and "fully understood" to convey the officer's action.

4) Select the most precise and clear sentence:

- a) The officer explained that the form needed to be filled out accurately.
- b) The officer said the form must be filled out properly and correctly.
- c) The officer emphasized the need to fill out the form with accuracy.
- d) The officer stated that the form has to be filled in a right manner.

Correct Answer: a) The officer explained that the form needed to be filled out accurately.
Explanation: Option (a) is straightforward and avoids redundancy, while communicating the requirement for accuracy.

Practice with Examples and Sample Questions
(D) Report Writing

1) Scenario: You are documenting an incident in which a traveler failed to declare agricultural products upon entry, leading to the confiscation of the items and a warning. Which summary is the most appropriate?

a) The traveler had agricultural items taken away, and they received a warning.
b) The traveler was found with undeclared agricultural items and was issued a warning.
c) The traveler declared agricultural products but was warned for failing to comply with regulations.
d) The traveler had agricultural products and was fined for failing to declare them.

Correct Answer:
b) The traveler was found with undeclared agricultural items and was issued a warning.
Explanation:
Option (b) is the most precise, stating both the issue (undeclared items) and the consequence (warning) without adding irrelevant information.

2) Scenario: You are preparing a report after discovering that a traveler attempted to smuggle a prohibited substance across the border. You can choose the most appropriate report summary.

a) The traveler was caught trying to smuggle items and was fined according to CBSA regulations.
b) The traveler attempted to smuggle illegal substances and was apprehended by CBSA officers.
c) CBSA officers caught the traveler smuggling prohibited substances and initiated legal actions.
d) A traveler was found to possess substances not allowed by the CBSA and was penalized.

Correct Answer:
c) CBSA officers caught the traveler smuggling prohibited substances and initiated legal actions.
Explanation:
Option (c) is the most detailed and accurate, clearly stating what was smuggled and the legal actions taken.

Practice with Examples and Sample Questions
(D) Report Writing

3) Scenario: While reviewing a traveler's luggage, you find counterfeit currency. What is the most appropriate way to summarize the incident in your report?

a) The traveler was caught with fake money and was charged.
b) The traveler had counterfeit currency in their possession, which was confiscated, and charges were filed.
c) Counterfeit currency was discovered in the traveler's luggage, leading to an investigation and charges.
d) The traveler attempted to cross the border with fake money and was arrested.

Correct Answer:
b) The traveler had counterfeit currency in their possession, which was confiscated, and charges were filed.
Explanation:
Option (b) provides a clear and direct summary, focusing on the possession of counterfeit currency and the resulting action (confiscation and charges).

4) Scenario: You are writing a report after a traveler failed to declare expensive electronics at the border and was fined for non-compliance. Choose the most appropriate summary.

a) The traveler was caught with undeclared electronics and received a fine for non-compliance.
b) The traveler didn't declare expensive electronics and was fined.
c) Undeclared electronics were discovered, and the traveler was fined according to CBSA policies.
d) The traveler declared expensive electronics and was fined for not following customs regulations.

Correct Answer:
a) The traveler was caught with undeclared electronics and received a fine for non-compliance.
Explanation:
Option (a) is clear and concise, providing the relevant details about the violation and the penalty.

Practice with Examples and Sample Questions
(E) Tone and Audience

1) You are writing a letter to a traveler denied entry into Canada due to incomplete documentation. What is the most appropriate tone?

a) Sympathetic and understanding
b) Formal and neutral
c) Aggressive and accusatory
d) Apologetic and informal

Correct Answer:
b) Formal and neutral
Explanation:
A formal and neutral tone is appropriate when dealing with official matters such as entry denial, as it maintains professionalism and avoids bias.

2) You are drafting an email to a colleague about an upcoming team meeting. What is the most appropriate tone?

a) Formal and distant
b) Friendly and casual
c) Strict and demanding
d) Apologetic and unsure

Correct Answer:
b) Friendly and casual
Explanation:
Since the email is directed to a colleague about an internal matter, a friendly and casual tone is more appropriate to foster open communication.

3) You need to write an internal report summarizing recent compliance statistics for senior management. Which tone is most suitable?

a) Formal and professional
b) Casual and conversational
c) Direct and critical
d) Apologetic and informal

Correct Answer:
a) Formal and professional
Explanation:
For an internal report intended for senior management, a formal and professional tone is expected to convey data accurately and authoritatively.

Practice with Examples and Sample Questions
(E) Tone and Audience

1) You are writing a letter to a traveler denied entry into Canada due to incomplete documentation. What is the most appropriate tone?

a) Sympathetic and understanding
b) Formal and neutral
c) Aggressive and accusatory
d) Apologetic and informal

Correct Answer:
b) Formal and neutral
Explanation:
A formal and neutral tone is appropriate when dealing with official matters such as entry denial, as it maintains professionalism and avoids bias.

2) You are drafting an email to a colleague about an upcoming team meeting. What is the most appropriate tone?

a) Formal and distant
b) Friendly and casual
c) Strict and demanding
d) Apologetic and unsure

Correct Answer:
b) Friendly and casual
Explanation:
Since the email is directed to a colleague about an internal matter, a friendly and casual tone is more appropriate to foster open communication.

3) You need to write an internal report summarizing recent compliance statistics for senior management. Which tone is most suitable?

a) Formal and professional
b) Casual and conversational
c) Direct and critical
d) Apologetic and informal

Correct Answer:
a) Formal and professional
Explanation:
For an internal report intended for senior management, a formal and professional tone is expected to convey data accurately and authoritatively.

Practice with Examples and Sample Questions
(E) Tone and Audience

4) A traveler has repeatedly ignored the customs regulations despite previous warnings. You are writing them a final warning letter. What tone should you use?

a) Formal but stern
b) Casual and indifferent
c) Polite and lenient
d) Humorous and light-hearted

Correct Answer:
a) Formal but stern

Explanation:
A formal but stern tone is appropriate in this scenario, as the traveler has repeatedly violated rules, and the seriousness of the situation must be conveyed.

5) You are writing an email to let a team member know they need to improve their performance. What would you say is the most appropriate tone?

a) Aggressive and forceful
b) Formal but encouraging
c) Casual and dismissive
d) Humorous and light-hearted

Correct Answer:
b) Formal but encouraging

Explanation:
Addressing performance issues requires a formal tone, but it should also encourage improvement rather than discourage the employee.

6) You are responding to a traveler's complaint about a delay they experienced at customs. Which tone is the most appropriate?

a) Apologetic and professional
b) Defensive and dismissive
c) Casual and informal
d) Strict and accusatory

Correct Answer:
a) Apologetic and professional

Explanation:
I think an apologetic and professional tone would be best for responding to a complaint, as it shows that the issue is being taken seriously while maintaining professionalism.

Practice with Examples and Sample Questions
(F) Proofreading and Editing

1) "The traveler was not aloud to cross the border due to improper documents." Which of the following is the correct revision?

a) Replace "aloud" with "allowed."
b) Replace "improper" with "incorrect."
c) Replace "was" with "were."
d) No errors.

Correct Answer:
a) Replace "aloud" with "allowed."
Explanation:
"Aloud" is a homophone of "allowed," but the correct term here is "allowed," meaning permitted.

2) "After questioning the traveller, the officer adviced him to fill out a declaration form." What is the correction?

a) Replace "adviced" with "advised."
b) Replace "fill out" with "complete."
c) Replace "traveller" with "traveler."
d) No errors.

Correct Answer:
a) Replace "adviced" with "advised."
Explanation:
"Adviced" is incorrect; the correct word is "advised," which is the past tense of "advise."

3) "The CBSA officer verified the documents and proceed to question the traveler." Which option corrects the error?

a) Replace "proceed" with "proceeded."
b) Replace "verified" with "verify."
c) Replace "question" with "questions."
d) No errors.

Correct Answer:
a) Replace "proceed" with "proceeded."
Explanation:
The correct past tense form of the verb "proceed" is "proceeded."

Practice with Examples and Sample Questions
(F) Proofreading and Editing

4) "The officer gave the traveller a verbal warning, he was cautioned to declare all items next time."

What is the correct edit?

a) Replace "gave" with "given."
b) Replace the comma with a semicolon.
c) Replace "cautioned" with "warned."
d) No errors.

Correct Answer:
b) Replace the comma with a semicolon.
Explanation:
This is a comma splice. The two independent clauses need to be separated by a semicolon.

5) "During the search, the officers found that the traveller had not declare several items of value."
Which correction is needed?

a) Replace "had not declare" with "had not declared."
b) Replace "found" with "finds."
c) Replace "value" with "valuable."
d) No errors.

Correct Answer:
a) Replace "had not declare" with "had not declared."
Explanation:
The correct past perfect form of the verb is "had not declared."

6) "The officer told the traveler to wait in the lobby until there name was called."
Which option fixes the error?

a) Replace "there" with "their."
b) Replace "was" with "is."
c) Replace "wait" with "waiting."
d) No errors.

Correct Answer:
a) Replace "there" with "their."
Explanation:
"Their" is the correct possessive pronoun; "there" refers to a place.

Practice with Examples and Sample Questions
(G) Document Completion

1) Document Information:
Traveler Name: John Smith
Nationality: Canadian
Incident: Attempted to bring undeclared tobacco products.
Which is the most appropriate summary for the incident report?

a) John Smith was caught smuggling tobacco and fined by CBSA.
b) John Smith, a Canadian citizen, was issued a warning for attempting to bring in undeclared tobacco products.
c) The traveler was fined for failing to declare tobacco products.
d) A Canadian national, John Smith, failed to declare tobacco products and was fined according to CBSA regulations.

Correct Answer:
d) A Canadian national, John Smith, failed to declare tobacco products and was fined according to CBSA regulations.

Explanation:
This answer provides the most complete and accurate information, including nationality and the fine according to CBSA regulations.

2) Document Information:
Traveler Name: Emily Watson
Nationality: British
Incident: Attempted to bring in restricted medications without a prescription.

Which is the most suitable summary of the incident?

a) Emily Watson, a British traveler, attempted to bring restricted medications and was detained.
b) Emily Watson was fined for not declaring her medications at the border.
c) A British traveler, Emily Watson, was fined for attempting to bring restricted medications without proper documentation.
d) The traveler, Emily Watson, was given a warning for bringing in medication without a prescription.

Correct Answer:
c) A British traveler, Emily Watson, was fined for attempting to bring restricted medications without proper documentation.

Explanation:
The answer clearly states the key points: nationality, the nature of the infraction, and the penalty issued.

Practice with Examples and Sample Questions
(G) Document Completion

3) Document Information:
Traveler Name: Carlos Rivera
Nationality: Mexican
Incident: Failed to declare $15,000 in cash, exceeding the allowable limit.
What is the most accurate summary for this report?

a) Carlos Rivera was caught smuggling large sums of money across the border.
b) A Mexican traveler, Carlos Rivera, was fined for failing to declare $15,000 in cash, exceeding the legal limit.
c) Carlos Rivera failed to declare a large sum of money and was fined.
d) The traveler was issued a warning for failing to declare money exceeding the limit.

Correct Answer:
b) A Mexican traveler, Carlos Rivera, was fined for failing to declare $15,000 in cash, exceeding the legal limit.

Explanation:
This option provides the most accurate and complete information about the traveler, the infraction, and the fine.

4) Document Information:
Traveler Name: Priya Kumar
Nationality: Indian
Incident: Attempted to bring in food items that are restricted.
Which summary best completes the report?

a) Priya Kumar, an Indian national, was fined for attempting to bring restricted food items into Canada.
b) Priya Kumar received a warning for attempting to import restricted food items.
c) A traveler was fined for trying to bring food into Canada.
d) Priya Kumar was stopped for attempting to bring restricted goods into Canada but was not fined.

Correct Answer:
a) Priya Kumar, an Indian national, was fined for attempting to bring restricted food items into Canada.

Explanation:
The answer includes the traveler's nationality, the nature of the violation, and the fine imposed.

7. Practice Test

(A) REASONING SKILLS PRACTICE QUESTIONS

1) Look at the following lists and find how many discrepancies are there:

List 1:
FT394567
MG562341
PL903218
WS198703
VL432509

List 2:
FT394567
MG562341
PL903218
WS198753
VL432509

(A) 0
(B) 1
(C) 2
(D) 3

2) Choose the following number in the following sequence: 7, 14, 9, 18, 11, 22, 13

(A) 26
(B) 28
(C) 24
(D) 30

3) Find the next number in the sequence: 2, 6, 12, 20, 30,….?

(A) 42
(B) 52
(C) 36
(D) 48

4) All oranges are fruits. All fruits grow on trees. Do you know which of the following statements is correct?

(A) Some oranges are not fruits
(B) All fruits are oranges
(C) Oranges grow on trees
(D) Fruits cannot be eaten

5) Choose the word that does not belong in this group: Shirt, Socks, Shoes, Tie

(A) Shirt
(B) Socks
(C) Shoes
(D) Tie

(A) REASONING SKILLS PRACTICE QUESTIONS

6) Find the number that completes this series: 3, 6, 12, 24, ...?

(A) 48
(B) 30
(C) 60
(D) 12

7) Which of the following numbers is not divisible by 3?

(A) 27
(B) 18
(C) 44
(D) 33

8) Which one of the following is a valid conclusion from this statement: "All artists are creative people"?

(A) Some artists are not creative people
(B) Some creative people are artists
(C) All creative people are artists
(D) No artists are creative people

9) Find the next number in the pattern: 1, 4, 9, 16,?

(A) 20
(B) 25
(C) 36
(D) 49

10) What is the odd: Apple, Banana, Orange, Carrot?

(A) Apple
(B) Banana
(C) Orange
(D) Carrot

11) Which word fits both these definitions? 1) A state of rest; 2) Something left behind after a battle

(A) Remains
(B) Peace
(C) Stillness
(D) Shadow

(A)REASONING SKILLS PRACTICE QUESTIONS

12) Find the next number in the sequence: 5, 8, 12, 17, ?

(A) 19
(B) 22
(C) 23
(D) 24

13) If every square is a rectangle and every rectangle is a polygon, which of the following is true?

(A) Every polygon is a square
(B) Some rectangles are squares
(C) Every polygon is a square
(D) No squares are polygons

14) If Lisa is taller than Sarah, and Sarah is taller than Mary, who is the tallest?

(A) Sarah
(B) Lisa
(C) Mary
(D) Cannot be determined

15) Which of the following best completes the analogy: Left is to the right as up is to:

(A) Top
(B) Over
(C) Down
(D) Side

16) A train leaves station A at 5:00 PM, traveling 80 km/h, and another leaves station B at 6:00 PM, traveling 100 km/h. If the distance between the stations is 400 km, when will they meet (closest option)?

(A) 8:00 PM
(B) 7:46 PM
(C) 9:00 PM
(D) 8:30 PM

(A)REASONING SKILLS PRACTICE QUESTIONS

17) Which shape does not belong in this group? Square, Triangle, Circle, Pentagon

(A) Square
(B) Triangle
(C) Circle
(D) Pentagon

18) Which word is a synonym for 'benevolent'?

(A) Kind
(B) Cruel
(C) Secretive
(D) Angry

19) Which of the following pairs completes the analogy: Fish is to water as bird is to:

(A) Earth
(B) Sky
(C) Nest
(D) Tree

20) If today is Wednesday, what day will it be five days from now?

(A) Monday
(B) Tuesday
(C) Thursday
(D) Friday

(B) ANALYTICAL THINKING PRACTICE QUESTIONS

Scenario Based Questions:

You act as a Border Services Officer (BSO) at a land border crossing. Your crossing has been selected for a high-profile event attended by government officials, including the Prime Minister, on November 7 at 1 pm. Multiple departments are involved in ensuring the event's success, and your supervisor has tasked you with handling incoming communications and assigning them priority levels based on the following criteria:

- Urgent/Important: This message needs to be addressed immediately. It is time-sensitive and critical to the event's success in terms of effectiveness, security, or the government's image.
- Urgent/Not important: This message should be addressed as soon as possible but is not critical to the event's success.
- Not urgent/Important: This message is not time-sensitive but must be addressed before the Prime Minister's arrival.
- Not urgent/Not important: This message must be more time-sensitive and critical to the event's success.

Question 1:

From: Paul Tanner, Transportation Logistics To: CBSA-ASFC
Date: November 6, 10:00 am
Subject: Delivery of Security Equipment
We will deliver the security equipment for the event today at 3 p.m. Please confirm where it should be delivered.
What is the priority of this message?

- A) Urgent/Important
- B) Urgent/Not important
- C) Not urgent/Important
- D) Not urgent/Not important

Question 2:

From: Alice Roberts, Catering Services
To: CBSA-ASFC
Date: November 5, 1:00 pm
Subject: Lunch Preferences for the Press
Could you provide me with any specific dietary restrictions for the event's press members?

What is the priority of this message?
- A) Urgent/Important
- B) Urgent/Not important
- C) Not urgent/Important
- D) Not urgent/Not important

(B) ANALYTICAL THINKING PRACTICE QUESTIONS

Question 3:

From: John Fisher, IT Support
To: CBSA-ASFC
Date: November 7, 9:00 am
Subject: Network Test for Live Stream
We must perform a final network test to ensure the live stream works. Can we access the media room at 10 a.m. today?

What is the priority of this message?
- A) Urgent/Important
- B) Urgent/Not important
- C) Not urgent/Important
- D) Not urgent/Not important

Question 4:

From: Sarah Thompson, Event Organizer
To: CBSA-ASFC
Date: November 4, 2:30 pm
Subject: Seating Arrangements for Officials
Please send me the final seating plan for the event's government officials.
What is the priority of this message?

- A) Urgent/Important
- B) Urgent/Not important
- C) Not urgent/Important
- D) Not urgent/Not important

Question 5:

From: Security Team
To: CBSA-ASFC
Date: November 6, 8:00 pm
Subject: Security Personnel Deployment
Could you confirm for us where our security personnel should be positioned for tomorrow's event? Please confirm by 8 am on November 7.
What is the priority of this message?

- A) Urgent/Important
- B) Urgent/Not important
- C) Not urgent/Important
- D) Not urgent/Not important

(B) ANALYTICAL THINKING PRACTICE QUESTIONS

Question 6:

From: David Lynch, Maintenance Services
To: CBSA-ASFC
Date: November 6, 3:00 pm
Subject: Heating System Check
We will be checking the heating system on the morning of November 7. Please confirm if this is acceptable.

What is the priority of this message?
- A) Urgent/Important
- B) Urgent/Not important
- C) Not urgent/Important
- D) Not urgent/Not important

Question 7:

From: Jane Phillips, Media Liaison
To: CBSA-ASFC
Date: November 7, 9:30 am
Subject: Parking Information for Media
We need to know where media vehicles will park for the press conference at 1 pm.

What is the priority of this message?
- A) Urgent/Important
- B) Urgent/Not important
- C) Not urgent/Important
- D) Not urgent/Not important

Question 8:

From: Victor Martinez, Janitorial Services
To: CBSA-ASFC
Date: November 5, 10:30 am
Subject: Cleaning Schedule Confirmation
Could you confirm the cleaning schedule for the event venue on November 7?

What is the priority of this message?
- A) Urgent/Important
- B) Urgent/Not important
- C) Not urgent/Important
- D) Not urgent/Not important

(B) ANALYTICAL THINKING PRACTICE QUESTIONS

Question 9:

From: Anne Lee, Audio-Visual Support
To: CBSA-ASFC
Date: November 6, 12:00 pm
Subject: Backup Equipment
We need confirmation on whether backup microphones and speakers are required for the press conference.

What is the priority of this message?
- A) Urgent/Important
- B) Urgent/Not important
- C) Not urgent/Important
- D) Not urgent/Not important

Question 10:

From: Oliver Jackson, Security Consultant
To: CBSA-ASFC
Date: November 6, 4:00 pm
Subject: Bomb Threat Procedures
Could you send over the bomb threat procedures in case we need to activate them during the Prime Minister's visit?

What is the priority of this message?
- A) Urgent/Important
- B) Urgent/Not important
- C) Not urgent/Important
- D) Not urgent/Not important

Logical Reasoning

11. A CBSA officer notices that passengers from a particular country are consistently flagged for additional screening. What can be inferred?

A) All passengers from that country should be screened.
B) The officer is biased.
C) There may be a legitimate security concern.
D) No specific pattern can be inferred.

(B) ANALYTICAL THINKING PRACTICE QUESTIONS

12. A vehicle approaches the border with a diplomatic plate. BSOs must ensure the driver adheres to regulations but cannot search the vehicle. What is the logical action?

- A) Let the vehicle through without any checks.
- B) Conduct a full search.
- C) Ensure identification and documentation are valid.
- D) Detain the driver for questioning.

Pattern Recognition

13. The pattern of passenger flow through a border crossing is 20, 50, 30, 60, 40. What is the next likely value?
- A) 70
- B) 80
- C) 50
- D) 90

Problem-Solving

14. A border crossing must process 200 vehicles in 4 hours, but after 2 hours, only 60 vehicles have been processed. How many cars must be processed per hour for the remaining time to meet the goal?
- A) 70
- B) 60
- C) 80
- D) 90

15. A CBSA officer must decide whether to increase patrols due to a 10% increase in passenger volume. What factor is most important to consider?
- A) Weather conditions.
- B) Number of available officers.
- C) Time of day.
- D) Length of the border crossing.

16. Due to an equipment failure, only half of the inspection booths at a border crossing are functional. What do you think is the best course of action?
- A) Close the border temporarily.
- B) Operate as usual with fewer booths.
- C) Reroute traffic to another crossing.
- D) Extend working hours for operational booths.

(B) ANALYTICAL THINKING PRACTICE QUESTIONS

Data Interpretation

17. According to the table, how much of the total traffic over the week occurred during the weekend? (Data: Sat: 400, Sun: 350, Mon-Fri: 1500 total)

- A) 20%
- B) 33%
- C) 40%
- D) 50%

18. If a pie chart shows that 25% of total inspections are for trucks, and the total number of inspections is 800, how many inspections are for trucks?
- (A) 150
- (B) 200
- (C) 250
- (D) 300

Situational Judgment

19. A CBSA officer receives a call from the mayor's office requesting a special favor for a relative crossing the border soon. What is the best course of action?
- A) Could you give the favor to maintain good relations?
- B) Ignore the request.
- C) Report the request to the supervisor.
- D) Comply only if the mayor insists.

20. The crossing is experiencing a technical issue that delays processing times. Passengers are becoming agitated. What do you think you should do?
A) Speed up processing without proper checks.
B) Close the crossing until the issue is resolved.
C) Communicate the situation to passengers and keep them updated.
D) Let passengers through without checks.

(C) CLIENT SERVICE ORIENTATION PRACTICE QUESTIONS

1) You have been tasked with reviewing a report from another team. While reviewing, you find that the data in the report do not align with previous records. What would be the most effective course of action?

- A) Make the necessary corrections and finalize the report without consulting the team.
- B) Compare the data with previous records and ask the team for clarification where discrepancies are found.
- C) Discard the report and request that the team redo the document.
- D) Approve the report as it is, assuming the discrepancies are minor.

2) You are reviewing a report with several sections, each drafted by a different team. One section contains data that is conflicting with the rest of the document. What do you think is the least effective way to handle this?

- A) Please correct the conflicting section without letting the team that drafted it know.
- B) Reach out to the team that drafted the conflicting section and ask for clarification on the data.
- C) Leave the conflict unresolved and submit the report as-is.
- D) Evaluate the conflicting section, offer recommendations for improvement, and provide feedback to the team.

3) You are finalizing a report when you notice that some data sources need to be correctly cited, which may affect the document's credibility. What would be the best way to address this issue?

- A) Submit the report. I hope that no one notices the missing citations.
- B) Go back and insert citations based on your understanding of the data.
- C) Notify the team responsible for the report and ask them to provide the missing citations.
- D) Remove the data altogether to avoid any complications.

4) You have been asked to finalize a presentation for your supervisor. Upon reviewing it, you notice that some visual aids (e.g., charts and graphs) are outdated and do not accurately reflect the current data. What would you say is the most effective response?

- A) Update the charts and graphs to reflect the latest data before finalizing the presentation.
- B) Ignore the outdated visuals and proceed with the presentation as it is.
- C) Remove the visual aids entirely to avoid potential confusion.
- D) Request another team to update the visuals for you without reviewing the new data.

(C) CLIENT SERVICE ORIENTATION PRACTICE QUESTIONS

5) You are reviewing a report that another team has completed. You notice that the report's tone could be more consistent across different sections. Some sections are highly formal, while others are more casual. What would be the least effective way to address this?

- A) Adjust the tone of the report yourself to ensure consistency throughout.
- B) Provide feedback to the team about the inconsistencies in tone and suggest revisions.
- C) Ignore the tone inconsistencies and submit the report as it is.
- D) Collaborate with the team to rewrite the sections using the appropriate tone.

6) You are assisting a family of four at the border. The parents do not speak English or French well, and the children seem frightened. How would you best help?

- A) Use simple language and speak louder to ensure they understand.
- B) Find a colleague who speaks their language or uses translation services.
- C) Ignore the language barrier and ask them to move along quickly.
- D) Hand them a brochure in English and point to the critical sections.

7) You are processing a large group of travelers. One individual insists that they urgently need to pass through, but their documentation needs to be completed. What do you do?

- A) Allow them to avoid confrontation.
- B) Process the other travelers first and review their documents thoroughly.
- C) Explain the importance of complete documentation and work with them to resolve it.
- D) Send them back to the line to wait until they find proper documents.

8) One of your colleagues is consistently short-tempered with travelers. This has resulted in complaints. How would you handle the situation?

- A) Ignore it; correcting a colleague is not your place.
- B) Confront your colleague immediately and tell them to change their behavior.
- C) Speak to your colleague privately and offer constructive feedback.
- D) Report your colleague to your supervisor without addressing it with them.

9) A traveler asks you several questions about entry requirements, but you are unsure of the answers. What would you do?

- A) Tell them to look it up online themselves.
- B) Guess based on what you think the answer might be.
- C) Inform them you will verify the information and get back to them.
- D) Redirect them to another officer without assistance.

(C) CLIENT SERVICE ORIENTATION PRACTICE QUESTIONS

10) You are reviewing a report that another team has completed. You notice that the report's tone could be more consistent across different sections. Some sections are highly formal, while others are more casual. What would be the least effective way to address this?

- A) Adjust the tone of the report yourself to ensure consistency throughout.
- B) Provide feedback to the team about the inconsistencies in tone and suggest revisions.
- C) Ignore the tone inconsistencies and submit the report as it is.
- D) Collaborate with the team to rewrite the sections using the appropriate tone.

11) You are processing travelers and encounter a family who seems confused about customs regulations. What would you do?

- A) Tell them to move aside and figure it out independently.
- B) Explain the customs regulations in detail and provide examples.
- C) Simply ask if they have any prohibited items and continue processing.
- D) Ask them to read the posted signs and proceed quickly.

12) During a busy period, you are asked to handle both the processing of travelers and assist with special event preparation. What do you think should be your priority?

- A) Focus on the particular event and handle travelers when you can.
- B) Balance both tasks equally, regardless of the workload.
- C) Prioritize processing travelers to maintain border efficiency.
- D) Delegate the travelers to someone else so you can focus on the event.

13) A traveler has a medical emergency while waiting in line. How do you think you could handle this situation?

- A) Call for medical assistance immediately and stay with the traveler.
- B) Tell them to move out of the line and wait for help.
- C) Ask another traveler if they can assist until help arrives.
- D) Ignore it and continue processing other travelers.

14) A new officer needs help to handle travelers during a busy shift and asks for your help. What would you do?

- A) Offer support and guidance while continuing to manage your tasks.
- B) Ignore the request and continue focusing on your work.
- C) Take over all their duties to avoid any delays.
- D) Report them to your supervisor for not being capable enough.

(C) CLIENT SERVICE ORIENTATION PRACTICE QUESTIONS

15) You receive an email from a traveler complaining about how they were treated at the border. What is your response?

- A) Apologize and ask for more details to resolve the situation.
- B) Ignore the email; travelers complain all the time.
- C) Defend the officer without investigating further.
- D) Forward the email to your supervisor without comment.

16) Question 11:
While working at a border crossing, you encounter a traveler needing help understanding the entry process. They are elderly and seem confused. What do you think the best approach is?

- A) Explain the process slowly and clearly, making sure they understand.
- B) Let them figure it out on their own.
- C) Ask them to step aside and return when ready.
- D) Have them wait for another officer to explain the process.

17) You are managing a busy shift, and a group of travelers arrives with questions about visa regulations. What do you do?

- A) Provide accurate information and direct them to the appropriate resources.
- B) Ask them to check the government website and move on.
- C) Tell them to ask someone else at a later time.
- D) Inform them you don't have time to answer their questions.

18) A supervisor asks you to help prepare a presentation for an upcoming meeting. However, you are already busy with other tasks. How would you be able to manage this situation?

- A) Inform your supervisor you're too busy and can't help.
- B) Help with the presentation, but rush through your other tasks.
- C) Prioritize your existing tasks and ask for an extension on the presentation.
- D) Delegate your other tasks to a colleague so you can focus on the presentation.

19) During a shift change, you notice that the officer replacing you needs to be made aware of some important updates during your shift. What should you do?

- A) Leave immediately; it's not your responsibility once your shift ends.
- B) Brief the officer quickly, even if it means staying a few minutes longer.
- C) Assume they'll find out from someone else later.
- D) Leave a note for them to read when they arrive.

20) A traveler becomes agitated after being selected for a secondary screening. How do you manage the situation?

- A) Explain the screening process calmly and provide reassurance.
- B) Ignore their agitation and proceed with the screening.
- C) Escalate the situation by calling in additional security.
- D) Apologize and allow them to skip the screening.

(D) WRITING SKILLS PRACTICE QUESTIONS

1) First, arrange the following words to form a complete sentence:
"will updated database be information tomorrow will for the the"
Second, from the choices below, please select the response option that includes the first letter of the second word followed by the last letter of the last word of the sentence.

- A) D N
- B) W N
- C) B W
- D) I E

2) First, arrange the following words to form a complete sentence:
"meeting the will held be at conference room the"
Second, from the choices below, please select the response option that includes the first letter of the fifth word followed by the last letter of the last word of the sentence.

- A) T M
- B) W N
- C) H M
- D) M E

3) Rearrange the following words to create a coherent sentence: "the report not will submit tomorrow he until checks grammar the." What is the correct arrangement?

- A) He will not submit the report until tomorrow the grammar checks.
- B) He will submit the report tomorrow until the grammar checks not.
- C) He will not submit the report until he checks the grammar tomorrow.
- D) The report checks the grammar until he will not submit tomorrow.

4) Which of the following sentences is grammatically correct?

- A) The officer, whom completed the report, left it on the supervisor's desk.
- B) The officer, who completed the report, left it on the supervisor's desk.
- C) The officer, that completed the report, left it on the supervisor's desk.
- D) The officer, whose completed the report, left it on the supervisor's desk.

5) Select the sentence that maintains clarity and precision:

- A) The document was proofread thoroughly by the editor, being someone who found mistakes, and fixed them before sending it out.
- B) The document was thoroughly proofread by the editor, who found and corrected the mistakes before sending it out.
- C) The editor, after proofreading the document, fixed mistakes in it and then after that sent it out.
- D) Proofread thoroughly, the document was sent out by the editor, which had some mistakes in it.

(D) WRITING SKILLS PRACTICE QUESTIONS

6) Which option best completes the sentence?
"Before submitting the final draft of the report, ensure that you _____."

- A) has reviewed it for clarity, grammatical correctness, and conciseness.
- B) have review it for clarity, grammatical correctness, and conciseness.
- C) reviewed it for clarity, grammatical correctness, and conciseness.
- D) have reviewed it for clarity, grammatical correctness, and conciseness.

7) Which of the following sentences uses appropriate tone and audience awareness for a formal report?

- A) Hey team, I went ahead and did that thing you asked me to do with the stats!
- B) The statistical analysis was completed as per your request and is attached for your review.
- C) Here's what I found, hope it helps you guys out. Let me know if it's cool.
- D) I made a few guesses with the data, but it should be mostly right. Please check.

8) Which of the following sentences is punctuated correctly?

- A) The report is due tomorrow however, we can ask for an extension if necessary.
- B) The report is due tomorrow; however, we can ask for an extension if necessary.
- C) The report is due tomorrow, however we can ask for an extension, if necessary.
- D) The report is due tomorrow: however we can ask for an extension if necessary.

9) Identify the sentence with correct subject-verb agreement:

- A) Each of the officers are responsible for submitting their reports on time.
- B) The team of officers is responsible for submitting their reports on time.
- C) Neither the officers nor the supervisor were at the meeting.
- D) The list of guidelines were updated for better clarity.

10) Which option best completes the sentence?
"After proofreading the report, I noticed that some sentences _____."

- A) was awkward and need revising.
- B) were awkward and needs revising.
- C) were awkward and needed revising.
- D) was awkward and needed revising.

11) Which sentence is written in the passive voice?

- A) The officer submitted the report yesterday.
- B) The report was submitted by the officer yesterday.
- C) The officer will submit the report tomorrow.
- D) The supervisor requested the report yesterday.

(D) WRITING SKILLS PRACTICE QUESTIONS

12) Choose the sentence with the correct parallel structure:

- A) The report is comprehensive, clear, and has precision.
- B) The report is comprehensive, clear, and precise.
- C) The report covers comprehensively, clarity, and precision.
- D) The report is comprehensive, has clarity, and is precise.

13) Which is the best revision for clarity and conciseness?
Original: "Due to the fact that the meeting was postponed until next week, the report will not be finalized by the end of this week."

- A) The report will not be finalized this week because the meeting was postponed until next week.
- B) The report, which was postponed until next week, will not be finalized by the end of this week.
- C) The report will not be finalized until next week as the meeting was postponed due to circumstances.
- D) Because the meeting was postponed until next week, the report will not be finalized by the end of this week.

14) Which sentence is correct?

- A) Neither the manager or the officers were responsible for the error.
- B) Neither the manager nor the officers were responsible for the error.
- C) Neither the manager nor the officers was responsible for the error.
- D) Neither the manager or the officers was responsible for the error.

15) Which of the following sentences demonstrates an appropriate formal tone for a business email?

- A) Hey, I just wanted to give you a heads-up about the changes in the report.
- B) I wanted to let you know that I made some changes to the report. Please review them.
- C) Just FYI, I made a few tweaks in the report. No big deal, but check it out when you get a chance.
- D) Yo, I made those changes you were asking for. Check it out.

16) Which option best completes the sentence? "Before finalizing the document, be sure that all _____."

- A) of the sources have been accurately cited.
- B) of sources has been accurately cited.
- C) sources are accurate, cited.
- D) sources was accurate and cited correctly.

(D) WRITING SKILLS PRACTICE QUESTIONS

17) Choose the sentence with correct punctuation:

- A) The officer completed the report quickly; but it still had several errors.
- B) The officer completed the report quickly but, it still had several errors.
- C) The officer completed the report quickly; however, it still had several errors.
- D) The officer completed the report quickly however it still had several errors.

18) Which of the following sentences is most concise?

- A. The reason why we went to the park was to play.
- B. We went to the park to play.
- C. In order to play, we went to the park.
- D. Playing, we went to the park.

19) Identify the sentence that contains a comma splice:

- A. The cat was purring, the dog was barking.
- B. I like to read books, especially science fiction.
- C. Because it was raining, we stayed home.
- D. The movie was long, but it was interesting.

20) Identify the sentence that uses active voice:

- A. The book was read by the student.
- B. The student read the book.
- C. The book was being read.
- D. The book will be read.

Practice Test Answers

REASONING SKILLS PRACTICE QUESTIONS

(1) Answer: (B) 1
Explanation:
A discrepancy is a difference or inconsistency between two sets of data.
Comparing List 1 and List 2, we can see that only one entry is different:
- WS198703 in List 1
- WS198753 in List 2

Therefore, there is only 1 discrepancy between the two lists.

2) Answer: (A) 26
Explanation:
- 7
- 7 * 2 = 14
- 7 + 2 = 9
- (7 + 2) * 2 = 18
- 7 + 2 + 2 = 11
- (7 + 2 + 2) * 2 = 22
- 7 + 2 + 2 + 2 = 13
- (7 + 2 + 2 + 2) * 2 = 26

So, the next number in the sequence is indeed 26.

3) Answer: (A) 42
Explanation:
Let's analyze the differences between consecutive terms:
- 6 - 2 = 4
- 12 - 6 = 6
- 20 - 12 = 8
- 30 - 20 = 10

Therefore, the following number in the sequence is 30 + 12 = 42.

4) Answer: (C) Oranges grow on trees
Explanation:
We are given two statements:
1. All oranges are fruits.
2. All fruits grow on trees.

Since all oranges are a subset of fruits, and all fruits grow on trees, it logically follows that oranges grow on trees.

5) Answer: (A) Shirt
Explanation:
- Shirts, socks, and shoes are all items of clothing worn on the lower part of the body.
- A tie is an accessory worn on the upper body.

Therefore, a shirt is odd as it fits a different category than the other three options.

(6) Answer: (A) 48
Explanation:
This is a geometric sequence where each number is double the previous one.
- 3 * 2 = 6
- 6 * 2 = 12
- 12 * 2 = 24

Following this pattern, the next number would be:
- 24 * 2 = 48

7) Answer: (C) 44
Explanation:
- A number is divisible by 3 if the sum of its digits is divisible by 3.
- For 44, the sum of the digits is 4 + 4 = 8, which is not divisible by 3.
- Therefore, 44 is not divisible by 3.

8) Answer: (B) Some creative people are artists
Explanation:
If all artists are creative, then it follows logically that some creative people must be artists. This is a valid deduction from the given statement.
The other options do not follow the given information logically.

9) Answer: (B) 25
Explanation:
The given sequence consists of the squares of consecutive natural numbers:
- $1 = 1^2$
- $4 = 2^2$
- $9 = 3^2$
- $16 = 4^2$

Following this pattern, the next number would be:
- $5^2 = 25$

10) Answer: (D) Carrot
Explanation:
- Apple, Banana, and Orange are all fruits.
- Carrot is a vegetable.

Therefore, carrot is the odd one out.

11) Answer: (A) Remains
- Remains can mean the state of being leftover or the parts of something left after the rest has gone.
- It can also refer to a state of rest or quietness.

REASONING SKILLS PRACTICE QUESTIONS

(12) Answer: (C) 23
Explanation:
The difference between consecutive numbers is increasing by 1 each time.
- 8 - 5 = 3
- 12 - 8 = 4
- 17 - 12 = 5

So, the next difference should be 6.
Therefore, the next number is 17 + 6 = 23.

13) Answer: (B) Some rectangles are squares
Explanation:
- Every square is a special type of rectangle, but not every rectangle is a square.
- Therefore, it's correct to say that some rectangles are squares.

14) Answer: (B) Lisa

If Lisa is taller than Sarah, and Sarah is taller than Mary, then Lisa is the tallest of the three.

15) Answer: (C) Down
Explanation:
- Left and right are opposites on a horizontal axis.
- Up and down are opposites on a vertical axis.

Therefore, "down" is the correct answer to complete the analogy.

16) Answer: (B) 7:46 PM
Explanation:

First train's journey:
It leaves at 5:00 PM.
So, by 6:00 PM, it would have traveled for 1 hour at 80 km/h, covering 80 km.
Remaining distance to cover = 400 km - 80 km = 320 km.
The combined speed of both trains:
- 80 km/h + 100 km/h = 180 km/h

Time taken to cover the remaining distance:
- Time = Distance / Speed = 320 km / 180 km/h = 16/9 hours = 1 hour and 46 minutes (approximately).
- Meeting time:

Both trains start moving towards each other at 6:00 PM. They will meet after 1 hour and 46 minutes.
So, they will meet at approximately 6:00 PM + 1 hour and 46 minutes = 7:46 PM.

(17) Answer: (C) Circle
Explanation:
- A square, triangle, and pentagon are all polygons, which are shapes with straight sides.
- A circle is a round shape with no sides.

18) Answer: (A) Kind
- Benevolent means kind, generous, and charitable.

19) Answer: (B) Sky
Explanation:
- A fish lives in water.
- A bird lives in the sky.

20) (A) Monday.
Explanation:
Today is Wednesday, and we need to find the day 5 days from now.
1. 1 day from Wednesday Thursday
2. 2 days from Wednesday: Friday
3. 3 days from Wednesday: Saturday
4. 4 days from Wednesday: Sunday
5. 5 days from Wednesday: Monday

ANALYTICAL THINKING PRACTICE QUESTIONS

Scenario Based Questions

1. A) Urgent/Important
- Explanation: The delivery of security equipment is time-sensitive and crucial to the success and security of the event.

2. C) Not urgent/Important
- Explanation: Although it's necessary for the event, this is not time-sensitive and can be taken care of before the Prime Minister's arrival.

3. A) Urgent/Important
- Explanation: I would like to inform you that ensuring the network functions correctly for the live stream is critical to the event's success and must be addressed immediately on the day of the event.

4. C) Not urgent/Important
- Explanation: The seating plan is vital for the event but not immediately time-sensitive. It can be addressed before the Prime Minister's arrival.

5. A) Urgent/Important
- Explanation: Security deployment is critical to the event's success and must be confirmed promptly. The message is both urgent and essential.

6. B) Urgent/Not important
- Explanation: While this needs to be addressed soon, it is not critical to the event's success. The heating system check is more of a logistical issue.

7. A) Urgent/Important
- Explanation: This is a critical logistical question for the press conference on the same day. It is essential to address it as soon as possible.

8. C) Not urgent/Important
- Explanation: While necessary for the event, the cleaning schedule is not urgent and can be confirmed before the Prime Minister's arrival.

9. B) Urgent/Not important
- Explanation: While this is somewhat urgent, it is only critical to the event's overall success if there are known technical issues.

10. A) Urgent/Important
Explanation: Bomb threat procedures are crucial to the safety and security of the event, and it is vital to ensure everyone is prepared for such a scenario.

(11) C) There may be a legitimate security concern.
Explanation:
While the officer may be biased, it's more likely that there's a legitimate security concern based on intelligence or past incidents involving passengers from that country. It's essential to avoid making assumptions based on stereotypes or prejudice.

12) Answer: C) Ensure identification and documentation are valid.
- Explanation:
While diplomatic vehicles have certain privileges, they are subject to some regulations. BSOs must verify the driver's identity and ensure they have the necessary documentation to cross the border. This includes checking their diplomatic status and any associated permits. However, a full search is not permitted due to diplomatic immunity.

13) Answer: A) 70
- Explanation:
The pattern seems to be an alternating increase and decrease by 30:
- 20 + 30 = 50
- 50 - 20 = 30
- 30 + 30 = 60
- 60 - 20 = 40

Following this pattern, the next value should be:
- 40 + 30 = 70

14) Answer: A) 70
Explanation:
- Total vehicles to be processed: 200
- Time remaining: 4 hours - 2 hours = 2 hours
- Vehicles already processed: 60
- Vehicles remaining to be processed: 200 - 60 = 140

To process 140 vehicles in 2 hours, the average rate must be:
- 140 vehicles / 2 hours = 70 vehicles per hour

15) Answer: B) Number of available officers.
Explanation:
While all factors could influence the decision, the most crucial consideration is the number of available officers. If there are more officers to handle the increased passenger volume, increasing patrols would be effective and could lead to longer wait times.

16) Answer: D) Extend working hours for operational booths.
Explanation:
While closing the border or rerouting traffic are options, they would likely cause significant disruptions and inconvenience to travelers. Extending the working hours of the operational booths would allow them to process more vehicles, minimizing the impact of the equipment failure.

ANALYTICAL THINKING PRACTICE QUESTIONS

Scenario Based Questions

17. B) 33 %
- Total traffic during the weekend: 400 + 350 = 750
- Total traffic for the week: 1500 + 750 = 2250
- Percentage of weekend traffic: (750 / 2250) * 100 = 33.33%

18..Answer: (B) 200
- Explanation:

To find 25% of 800, we can multiply 800 by 0.25:
- 800 * 0.25 = 200

Therefore, 200 inspections are for trucks.

19. Answer: C) Report the request to the supervisor.
- Explanation:

While it's important to maintain good relations with local officials, granting special favors can compromise the integrity of the CBSA's operations and create a perception of favoritism. Reporting the request to the supervisor ensures that the incident is documented and that appropriate steps can be taken to address the situation.

20) Answer: C) Communicate the situation to passengers and keep them updated.

Explanation:

While closing the crossing or letting passengers through without checks might seem like quick solutions, they could lead to more significant problems. The best course of action is to communicate the situation to passengers and keep them updated. This helps maintain transparency, reduces frustration, and allows passengers to plan accordingly.

CLIENT SERVICE ORIENTATION PRACTICE QUESTIONS

(1) Answer: (B) Compare the data with previous records and ask the team for clarification where discrepancies are found.
Explanation: The most effective response is to clarify discrepancies with the team while cross-referencing previous records to ensure accuracy and accountability in the report.

2) Answer: (C) Leave the conflict unresolved and submit the report as-is.
Explanation: Leaving the conflict unresolved compromises the accuracy of the entire report and does not address the root cause of the issue, making this the least practical approach.

3) Answer:(C) Notify the team responsible for the report and ask them to provide the missing citations.
Explanation: The best approach is communicating with the team responsible for ensuring that citations are added to maintain the report.

4) Answer:(A) Update the charts and graphs to reflect the latest data before finalizing the presentation.
Explanation: Accurately representing current data in visual aids is essential for clear and effective communication during presentations.

5) Answer: (C) Ignore the tone inconsistencies and submit the report as it is.
Explanation: Ignoring tone inconsistencies can negatively impact the clarity and professionalism of the report, making this the least practical course of action.

6) Answer: (B) Find a colleague who speaks their language or uses translation services.
Explanation: Ensuring they fully understand the situation is the most effective way to provide quality service while respecting their needs.

7) Answer: (C) Explain the importance of complete documentation and work with them to resolve the issue.
Explanation: Balancing urgency with correct procedure ensures good client service and compliance with regulations.

8) Answer:(C) Speak to your colleague privately and offer constructive feedback.
Explanation: giving constructive feedback directly to your colleague encourages improvement while maintaining a positive working environment.

9) Answer:(C) Inform them you will verify the information and get back to them.
Explanation: Ensuring accurate information is provided, even if it takes extra time, and maintaining high service standards.

10) Answer: (C) Provide detailed feedback with recommendations for improvement.
Explanation: Providing specific feedback fosters improvement and collaboration between departments.

(11) Answer: (B) Explain the customs regulations in detail and provide examples.
Explanation: Providing clear, helpful information ensures that travelers comply with regulations and feel supported.

(12) Answer: (C) Prioritize processing travelers to maintain border efficiency.
Explanation: Ensuring the smooth processing of travelers takes precedence to prevent delays and maintain border security.

13) Answer:(A) Call for medical assistance immediately and stay with the traveler.
Explanation: Ensuring the safety and well-being of the traveler is a top priority in this situation.

14) Answer: (A) Offer support and guidance while continuing to manage your tasks.
Explanation: Providing support while balancing your responsibilities demonstrates leadership and teamwork.

15) Answer: (A) Apologize and ask for more details to resolve the situation.
Explanation: Acknowledging the complaint and seeking further information shows a commitment to resolving issues and maintaining good service.

16) Answer: A) Explain the process slowly and clearly, ensuring they understand.
Explanation: Taking the time to ensure the traveler understands demonstrates empathy and vital client service.

17) Answer: C) The officer completed the report quickly; however, it still had several errors.

Explanation: The semicolon properly separates two independent clauses, and "however" is correctly punctuated with commas.

18) C) Prioritize your existing tasks and ask for an extension on the presentation.
Explanation: Managing priorities and communicating effectively with your supervisor ensures that all tasks are completed with quality.

19) B) Brief the officer quickly, even if it means staying a few minutes longer.
Explanation: Ensuring a smooth handover by briefing the next officer promotes continuity and service quality.

20) A) Explain the screening process calmly and provide reassurance.
Explanation: A calm explanation can help diffuse tension and promote understanding, ensuring a smoother process.

WRITING SKILLS PRACTICE QUESTIONS

(1) Answer: (A) D N
Explanation: The correct sentence is: "The database will be updated tomorrow for the information." The first letter of the second word is "D" (database), and the last letter of the last word is "N" (information).

2) Answer: (C) H M
Explanation: The correct sentence is: "The meeting will be held at the conference room." The first letter of the fifth word is "H" (held) and the last letter of the last word is "M" (room).

3) Answer: (C) He will not submit the report until he checks the grammar tomorrow.
Explanation: The sentence is structured logically, with clear subject-verb agreement and chronological order.

4) Answer:(B) The officer, who completed the report, left it on the supervisor's desk.
Explanation: "Who" is the correct pronoun when referring to a person (the officer) as the subject of the relative clause.

5) Answer: (B) The document was thoroughly proofread by the editor, who found and corrected the mistakes before sending it out.
Explanation: This sentence is clear, concise, and maintains a logical flow.

6) Answer: (D) have reviewed it for clarity, grammatical correctness, and conciseness.

Explanation: The sentence requires the correct present perfect verb tense "have reviewed" to indicate the action completed before submission.

7) Answer: (B) The statistical analysis was completed as per your request and is attached for your review.
Explanation: The sentence maintains a professional tone and addresses the audience with respect and formality, which is suitable for a report.

8) Answer:(B) The report is due tomorrow; however, we can ask for an extension if necessary.
Explanation: The semicolon properly separates two independent clauses, and "however" is correctly punctuated with commas.

9) Answer:(B) The team of officers is responsible for submitting their reports on time.
Explanation: "Team" is a collective noun, so the singular verb "is" is correct. The sentence maintains proper subject-verb agreement.

10) Answer:(C) were awkward and needed revising.
Explanation: The subject "sentences" is plural, so the verbs "were" and "needed" must both be in agreement.

11) Answer:(B) The report was submitted by the officer yesterday.
Explanation: Passive voice occurs when the subject of the sentence receives the action rather than performs it.

(12) Answer: (B) The report is comprehensive, clear, and precise.
Explanation: This sentence maintains a parallel structure by using adjectives in a series.

13) Answer:(A) The report will not be finalized this week because the meeting was postponed until next week.
Explanation: This revision simplifies the sentence, maintaining clarity and eliminating unnecessary words.

14) Answer: (B) Neither the manager nor the officers were responsible for the error.
Explanation: "Neither... nor" correctly pairs with plural "officers" and the plural verb "were."

15) Answer: (B) I wanted to let you know that I made some changes to the report. Please review them.
Explanation: This sentence maintains professionalism while clearly communicating the necessary information

16) Answer: A) of the sources have been accurately cited.
Explanation: The subject "sources" is plural, so the verb "have been" must agree in number, and the phrase is grammatically correct.

17) Answer: A) Provide accurate information and direct them to the appropriate resources.
Explanation: Offering accurate information and guidance ensures that travelers are well-informed and supported.

18) Answer: B. We went to the park to play.
Explanation: This sentence is the most concise because it directly states the action without unnecessary words.

19) Answer: A. The cat was purring, the dog was barking.
Explanation: A comma splice occurs when two independent clauses are joined only by a comma. In this sentence, "The cat was purring" and "the dog was barking" are complete sentences, but they are only separated by a comma. To correct this, you could add a conjunction like "and" or "but."

20) Answer: B. The student read the book.
Explanation: In active voice, the subject performs the action. In this sentence, the student is the subject and is performing the action of reading the book.

CONCLUSION

Congratulations on completing OTEE PRACTICE TEST AND STUDY GUIDE FOR CBSA)Master the Canadian Border Services OTEE CBSA Exams with Comprehensive Practice Tests and Study Strategies! By reaching this point, you have taken a significant step toward mastering the skills and knowledge required for success in the OTEE and, ultimately, your future as a Canadian Border Services Officer.

The journey to becoming a Border Services Officer is both challenging and rewarding. Through the practice tests, study strategies, and guidance in this book, you have equipped yourself with the analytical thinking, reasoning skills, and client service orientation needed to excel in this demanding role. Remember that success in the OTEE is not solely about memorizing information but understanding how to apply these skills effectively in real-life scenarios.

As you continue to prepare for the exam, stay focused and regularly revisit the concepts and practice exercises. Consider the exam an opportunity to demonstrate your readiness for the responsibilities and challenges ahead. Your ability to analyze complex situations, think critically, and make sound judgments will help you succeed on the test and be invaluable throughout your career in protecting Canada's borders.

We hope this guide has been an essential tool in your preparation and has boosted your confidence in taking the next step. Stay determined, keep refining your skills, and trust in the effort you've put into your studies.

Best of luck with your OTEE exam and future career with the CBSA!

You've got this!

EXAM PREP MASTERY - DR. FANATOMY

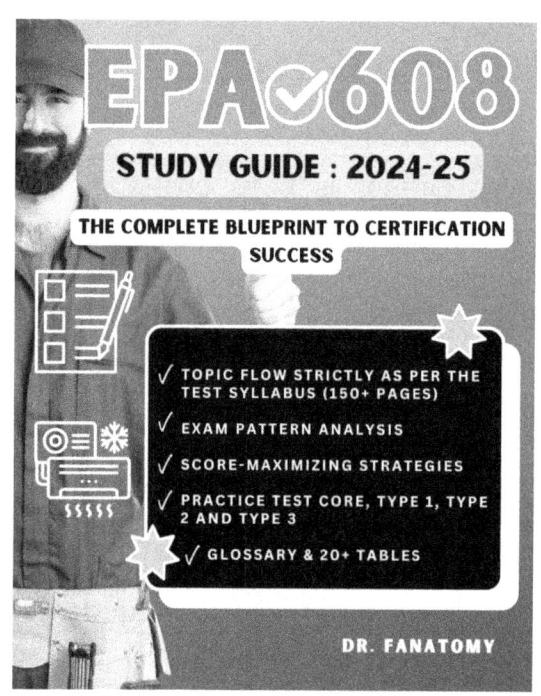

www.ingramcontent.com/pod-product-compliance
Lightning Source LLC
Chambersburg PA
CBHW082210070526
44585CB00020B/2354